THE OFFICIAL *Vince Lombardi* PLAYBOOK

THE OFFICIAL
VINCE LOMBARDI
PLAYBOOK

✗ HIS CLASSIC PLAYS & STRATEGIES

✗ PERSONAL PHOTOS & MEMENTOS

✗ RECOLLECTIONS FROM FRIENDS
   & FORMER PLAYERS

PHIL BARBER
FOREWORD BY VINCE LOMBARDI JR.

The Lyons Press
Guilford, Connecticut
An imprint of The Globe Pequot Press

The Lyons Press is an imprint of The Globe Pequot Press.

The Official Vince Lombardi Playbook is produced by becker&mayer!, Bellevue, Washington.
www.beckermayer.com

Design: Kasey Free
Editorial: Amy Wideman
Photo Research: Chris Campbell
Production Coordination: Leah Finger
License Acquisition: Josh Anderson

Library of Congress Cataloging-in-Publication Data is available on file.

ISBN 978-1-59921-536-5

Printed in China
10 9 8 7 6 5 4 3 2 1

CONTENTS

ABOVE The Lombardis at home in Fairhaven, New Jersey, when he was named coach of the Packers in 1959: Vince, Marie, Vince Jr. (17) and Susan (12).

FOREWORD by Vince Lombardi Jr.

I've always been struck by the contrast between the NFL Championship Games of 1966 and 1967. They were almost exactly a year apart, and both were confrontations between the Dallas Cowboys and my father's team, the Green Bay Packers. The Packers were established as the team to beat in the NFL. The Cowboys were ascending.

The games ended in eerily similar situations. But with very different outcomes.

In the '66 title game, Dallas had a first down at the Green Bay 2-yard line with 1:52 left, but couldn't put it in—partly due to a mental error, a false start that pushed the ball back five yards.

Flash-forward 364 days. Sixteen seconds left, ball at the Cowboys' 1-yard line. This time it was the Packers' turn to score or leave the field in defeat, and faced with almost a mirror image, they were able to put it in.

Over the years, I began to wonder what separated the two teams. Why did the Packers succeed where the Cowboys failed when the rivals seemed so evenly matched? Part of it was experience. Tom Landry's Dallas team was still young; my father's team was loaded with players who had already won three NFL championships.

But I believe a lot of it came down to preparation and resolve. I never watched the Cowboys practice, but I know there was as much pressure at a Packers practice as there was during a game—the pace, the intensity, the criticism.

At the end of each practice, for example, the offense would work on getting off the ball quickly on the snap. My father thought the key was to fire out as a single unit—not, as he would say, like a bunch of typewriter keys. If they didn't do it right, he'd say "run it again." They had to run 20 to 30 yards downfield each time, so it got old pretty fast.

By my father's third year in Green Bay, he didn't have to say a word after a bad start. The players would know, and they'd be the ones to say "run it again." They were collectively holding themselves accountable, and that's when you make the quantum leap to being a great team.

The Packers had enough talent to make it to six NFL title games in nine years. But it was poise, discipline, and something my father called mental toughness that allowed them to win five of those games, and that is what really made my father proud.

INTRODUCTION Right Coach, Right Place, Right Time

It's hard to say whether Vince Lombardi was more revered in life or after his death. Calling Lombardi a living legend in the 1960s was no exaggeration. The Packers were downtrodden when Lombardi arrived in Green Bay in 1959. The city was waiting for a hero, and it arrived in the form of a squat, emotional, occasionally corny football coach.

Within four years, Lombardi had guided his team to two NFL championships and become one of the most recognizable figures in sports. As the Packers rolled to additional titles in 1965, 1966, and 1967, his persona grew outsize. America was coming apart at the seams, torn by war, protest, racial discord, and a general polarization of lifestyles. Many saw Lombardi's conservative demeanor and obsession with

discipline as the route home to a steadier time, as ballast for a ship suddenly teetering in the waves.

Football fans flocked to Lombardi, but they weren't the only ones.

He was constantly on the public-speaking circuit in the off-season, addressing businessmen and civic organizations on the importance of loyalty, sacrifice, excellence, and determination. Someone shot a motivational business film in which the coach turns a sad-sack salesman into a dynamo. By 1968, Republican presidential candidate Richard Nixon was seriously looking at Lombardi as a running mate. Nixon was sorry to find that the coach was closely aligned with the Kennedy family, and had in fact joined a

ABOVE The triumphant Packers carry Coach Lombardi from the field.

group of sports figures pushing for gun control in the wake of Robert Kennedy's assassination.

A year later, Lombardi took Washington, D.C., by storm, but as a football coach. A year after that, Lombardi was dead, a victim of colon cancer.

Few of the football figures from the 1960s remain household names. Some are practically forgotten by mainstream culture. Lombardi, on the other hand, seems almost to be enjoying a public afterlife.

Sure, there are the local reminders of his glory days: Lombardi Way, one of the streets bordering Lambeau Field in Green Bay, and a 14-foot statue of Lombardi outside the stadium. A more visible national reminder is the symbol of NFL dominance—the Vince Lombardi Trophy, as the Super Bowl trophy was renamed. But it isn't just the civic proclamations. His name still resonates in the public mind. It is still associated with effort, toughness, dignity, and, above all, success.

As Forrest Gregg, his old offensive lineman, says: "Everyone wants to know what Vince Lombardi was really like—young people you'd think would have no idea who Vince Lombardi was. He passed away many years ago. Yet they still know him."

Perhaps it's because unlike most coaches, Lombardi didn't stick around long enough to lose. He won every year he coached, making it seem as though he could have done it forever if only the disease hadn't cut him down early. And who knows, maybe he could have.

Most of the men who played for him will you tell you that Lombardi's winning ways were anything but chance. They saw the organization he built from the executive office down to the practice field, how he envisioned a plan and enacted it through the sheer force of his will.

There are many explanations for Lombardi's success as a coach. He had a keen memory, an analytical mind, and a passionate love of football. He was headstrong and tireless, determined to get his way and to come up with solutions to strategic problems. He was charismatic in his way, a man

whom people naturally feared and at the same time admired. Like the John Wooden of football, he was known for his homilies and slogans, many of them posted on signs in the locker room. They would probably be dismissed as preachy today; at the time, they made him seem wise.

But there's one factor that shouldn't be overlooked when breaking down Vince Lombardi's strengths: his playbook.

Not that it was a particularly complex or fanciful document. Just the opposite. Lombardi's playbook was a model of simplicity, a relatively small collection of sheets—maybe an inch and a half thick, where those of other coaches could be four inches—that changed only a little between 1959 and 1967. But it was built on his astute observations of the game, and it became the standard.

"I can almost go page by page," former quarterback Zeke Bratkowski says, peering back through the decades. "It was the length of about a legal pad, green, with a very flexible cover. Obviously it had tabs—you know, by topic, starting with basic information, formations, cadence—then got into definition of defenses and so forth."

Lombardi wouldn't simply hand his athletes a full playbook each summer. Rather, he would start at the beginning—a painfully deliberate process for some of the veterans—and the players were expected to copy the plays for themselves

ABOVE Fans turn out to help the coach dedicate Lombardi Avenue in Green Bay.

ABOVE Lombardi during the 1966 NFC Championship Game in Dallas. In the foreground is halfback Donny Anderson.

as he scribbled on a chalkboard. "You were responsible for drawing everything up as he drew it up on the board," former receiver Boyd Dowler says. "He'd draw up plays against different fronts and coverages. And in longhand, he'd give you different coaching points. You learned it by doing it."

In meetings every day, his offensive players would insert another page, additional packages of runs or passes. The defense went through a similar process, though their playbooks were simpler and less hallowed. At the end of the year, the players would give the pages back, lest they leave the team and be tempted to offer up Lombardi's plays to an opponent.

During the season, the Packers carried these playbooks around like dog-eared, coffee-stained bibles, studying them in the evenings and turning them into flesh-and-blood plays on the practice field. "I can tell you any defense they play, how to block it. Still," says former tight end Ron Kramer, who predated Lombardi in Green Bay by two seasons. "If I call

Bart Starr on the phone and say, 'Bart, call a play,' he might go, 'Brown Right, A & B Circle, Left Fly.' That means the two backs circle and the left end flies. I can still remember like it was yesterday. And that's mostly due to Vince Lombardi's thoroughness, because I don't remember the other two years."

Lombardi's terminology was simple and stable. He used colors to denote formations—Brown meant the fullback was stationed directly behind the quarterback, for instance, while Red meant split backs—a system he brought with him from his days as an assistant with the New York Giants. "I was such a nut," Kramer says. "I'd mark all the Red Right plays in red, the Blue Right plays in blue, the Green Right plays in green. When I went through my book, I didn't have to look at where the positions were."

Lombardi's numbering system on running plays was just as basic: one number for the ball carrier, another for the hole. If Starr called 43 Double Pinch, the 4 back would run

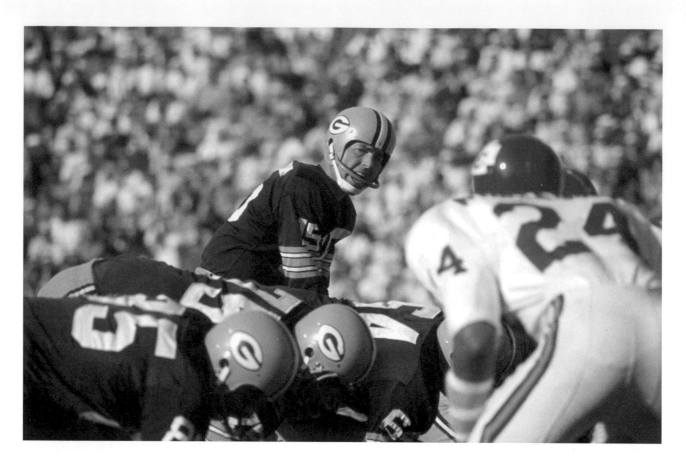

through the 3 hole. Double Pinch defined a blocking pattern. At the beginning of Lombardi's first season, 2 stood for the left halfback, 3 for the fullback and 4 for the right halfback. He soon changed to a two-back system, and thereafter used 2 for the fullback and 4 for the halfback.

As for the holes, the number increased as the play got farther from the center. Odd-numbered plays were to the right, even numbers to the left—to the lasting befuddlement of those Packers who remained in the NFL after their playing days. "When I got into coaching, the playbooks had it even to the right, odd to the left," Bratkowski says. "To this day I can't look at a formation and say 'the 6 hole off the right.' It's a glitch for me."

Dowler can sympathize. "I had to call plays for the Cincinnati Bengals," he says. "I'd be standing around in practice, I'd call a certain play and be looking in the wrong direction."

Any words in the play call tended to refer to blocking assignments or pass routes. "Easy" told an end to block the outside linebacker on his side. "Take" put a tackle on the outside linebacker. "Snapper" meant the center blocked a linebacker. It was a welcome simplification over the Packers' previous system of terminology. "In the years before Lombardi, the quarterback came into the huddle and he might call '49 B-O Pop George Greg,'" Kramer says. "That means the on-guard pulls, the off-guard pulls. B is 'the back blocks.' The quarterback had to call everybody's block. It made it so complicated, it was unbelievable."

Imagine communicating those long strings of words under the ticking pressure of a two-minute drill. Instead of making the quarterback verbalize all the assignments, Lombardi diffused responsibility to all eleven players. The quarterback would say one word, and the other ten had to know their splits

ABOVE Quarterback Bart Starr calls signals during Super Bowl I, the January 15, 1967, matchup with Kansas City.

or blocking responsibilities on the play. "So Bart could come in and say, 'OK, Red Right 49 on two,'" Kramer explains.

"It gave us the responsibility of knowing the whole play," Dowler says. "We had better knowledge of the big picture, rather than, 'All I have to worry about is what I'm doing.' It gave us ownership of the offense, so to speak."

Lombardi really foisted just one fundamental change on his offense. With his team struggling in 1959, the first-year head coach went from a three-back base set to a two back set, converting one halfback into a flanker. The result was much more like the offenses we see today. Other than that, a player like Starr who stuck around for all of Lombardi's nine seasons in Green Bay saw little change to his offense. "He'd start from the beginning every year, with just as much enthusiasm as the last year," Dowler notes. "But if he said one thing one year that was a little different, it would get your attention."

Lombardi never felt that "out-coaching" an opponent meant coming up with a play they'd never seen before. Rather, he wanted his players to be technically sound, maybe even perfect, in the limited number of plays they ran. "Some people try to find things in this game or put things into it which don't exist," Lombardi once said. "Football is two things. It's blocking and tackling. I don't care anything about formations or new offenses or tricks on defense. You block and tackle better than the team you're playing, you win."

The Packers had trick plays like any other team, end-arounds and double passes. They just didn't use them much. "I don't know how many reverses we ran in nine years," Dowler says. "I know I ran two. If we ran five, I'd be surprised. We didn't run trick plays. We ran plays that complemented one another, plays like the sweep and the run trap."

Lombardi's offensive system was sort of a contradiction. His playbook was minimalist. But most plays had built-in options for just about every player, depending on how the defense reacted. "It was a simplified-complicated game," Bratkowski says. "That's about the best description I could give."

The Packers drove opponents crazy. Defensive coaches would break down their film and see that Lombardi wasn't doing anything too innovative. Yet no one could stop him. "I knew a lot of guys from Texas," says Dowler. "The Cowboys had all this computer stuff. I'd hear, 'You can line up in split backs, and we know what you do.' Finally I'd say, 'Yeah, well do something about it.' We weren't tricking anybody."

It wasn't necessarily that the Packers had better talent, though their talent was pretty good (thanks in part to Lombardi's personnel assessments). It wasn't that they "wanted it more," a common refrain in sports that is usually meaningless. The key was repetition. Rookies would come in first each summer to begin their indoctrination into the Lombardi system and the playbook. The veterans would show up maybe a week later, and they, too, would start from scratch.

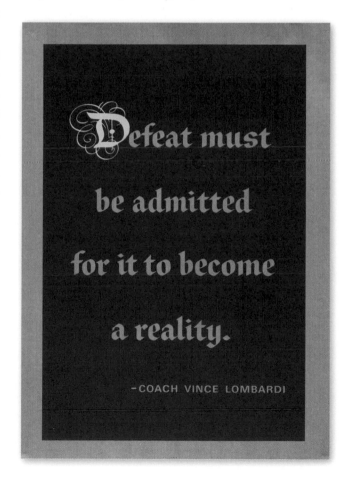

Defeat must be admitted for it to become a reality.

– COACH VINCE LOMBARDI

ABOVE Lombardi's offices and locker room were dotted with his favorite aphorisms, attached to the wall on plaques and placards.

13

Lombardi would hold up a ball and proclaim, 'Gentlemen, this is a football.'"

And wide receiver Max McGee, the designated cut-up, would pipe up and say, "Slow down, would ya, Coach? You're going too fast." Then the frivolity would be over and the Packers would set about learning the playbook from A to Z. More important, they would practice the plays endlessly, until they became reflexive.

"We may not know any more about football than most of the other coaches in the league," Lombardi once said, according to Bob Rubin's *Green Bay Packers Return to Glory*. "But if we can put everything we know together so it makes good basic sense and then drill-drill-drill it into them . . . that kind of coaching can make winners out of losers."

And no one could drill-drill-drill like Lombardi. He taught high school physics, chemistry, and Latin for eight years at St. Cecilia High School in Englewood, New Jersey. His teaching philosophy, like his coaching philosophy, was to explain everything to the lowest student in the class, or player on the team, and he wouldn't move on to the next point until everyone understood. He used the same thorough, structured approach when he took over the Packers, breaking down his offense in minute detail first for his assistant coaches, then his players.

"He was famous or infamous for his adages on winning, and whether it was the most important thing," former center Bill Curry says. "He was famous for his records, and for his fire and his profanity and his demanding approach to the game. But not as much for what he did best. What a great teacher does is make you want to please him or her. I'll never forget what he taught me. That was his greatest gift."

And it's a gift that has never gone bad or expired or fallen out of style. Lombardi taught his disciples, and they taught theirs, and his philosophies of football and life have passed through a generation or three. In a way, anyone who loves football has been a beneficiary.

ABOVE The coach goes over plays with the Giants (top) and instructs kicker Don Chandler (bottom). **OPPOSITE** Lombardi on the sidelines.

MAKING OF A COACH

LOMBARDI BEFORE GREEN BAY

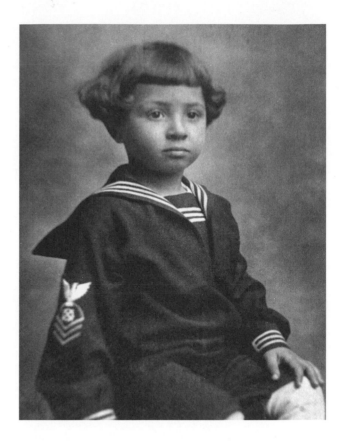

When team president Dominic Olejniczak recommended Vince Lombardi as the next coach of the Green Bay Packers in 1959, committee member John Torinus reportedly asked, "Who the hell is Vince Lombardi?"

It was a fair inquiry. Lombardi was a respected assistant for the New York Giants, but few outside of the inner circle of the National Football League had heard of him when the Packers made him the sixth head coach in franchise history. Yet he was, in many ways, completely prepared for the job. Lombardi's upbringing, and especially his early career in sports, provided him with the structure, the football philosophy, the practice methods and the plays that would help propel the Packers to greatness.

Vince Lombardi was born in the Sheepshead Bay neighborhood in southeast Brooklyn on June 11, 1913. His father, Harry Lombardi, was a squat, powerful meat wholesaler who had emigrated from Italy and went by the nickname Tattoos—a reference to the ink that covered both his arms. Written on the fingers of one hand, one letter to each finger, was the word WORK; on the other hand was the word PLAY. Vince's mother was born Matilda Izzo. Her family was huge, close-knit, and part of the cultural weave of Sheepshead Bay. Vince had two younger sisters, Madeline and Claire, and two younger brothers, Harold and Joseph, and the Lombardis spent many weekends eating, drinking, and socializing at the boisterous home of Matilda's parents on East 16th Street, the house where Vince was born.

As a boy, Vince seriously considered joining the priesthood. That notion later seemed laughable to his players, who saw more than they wanted of the coach's profane side, but Lombardi would remain a devout Catholic. While coaching the Packers, David Maraniss noted in *When Pride Still Mattered*, he prayed to St. Anthony and St. Jude in his bedroom every morning. And he attended mass seven days a week at St. Willebrord's Church in Green Bay, an old Dutch Catholic church run by the Norbertines, before heading to work. He maintained his routine on the road, too. "It's the only way I can control my terrible temper," he confided to friends. He kept rosary beads in his coat pocket, and another set in the car. As his quarterback Bart Starr was fond of saying, "If you

OPPOSITE Lombardi in uniform for the Fordham Rams. **ABOVE** Vincent Thomas Lombardi, born June 11, 1913, in Brooklyn.

17

STALCUP LOMBARDI

GIFT

CISBELL

heard Coach Lombardi at practice every afternoon, you knew why he had to go to church every morning."

Lombardi attended Cathedral College of the Immaculate Conception, a diocesan seminary in Brooklyn, but left before completing its six-year program. He got cold feet about the priesthood, no doubt, but also found himself missing football. After transferring to St. Francis Preparatory School, also in Brooklyn, he played a season as fullback on the football team, and he also played basketball and baseball and ran track.

After high school, Lombardi moved on to Fordham University in the Bronx. He was recruited by Jimmy Crowley, left halfback among the legendary Four Horsemen of Notre Dame and who, ironically, grew up in Green Bay.

These were among the glory years of Lombardi's life, and they cemented his love for football. He was one on Fordham's celebrated "Seven Blocks of Granite," a two-way line for one of the 1930s' college-football powers. Most of the seven blocks soon disappeared into obscurity, though Alex Wojciechowicz played thirteen seasons as a center and linebacker with the

ABOVE Lombardi pursues a Purdue ball carrier while playing for Fordham. Cecil Isbell would later start for the Packers.

Detroit Lions and Philadelphia Eagles, and was one of the finest players of his generation. Lombardi, known as Vinnie in those days, was a 172-pound guard, tough and scrappy but nothing like the best player on the team. He was a committed student who made the Dean's list and earned a bachelor's degree in 1937.

After graduation, Lombardi studied nights at Fordham University Law School and worked days as an insurance investigator. At one point he worked at DuPont for $20 a week. On weekends he suited up for the Brooklyn Eagles or the Wilmington Clippers of the semi-pro American Association.

It was in 1939 that he took his first coaching job, signing on as an assistant football coach at St. Cecilia High School in Englewood, New Jersey. He also taught physics, chemistry, and Latin, and made $1,700 a year. He married Marie Planitz in 1940.

At St. Cecilia, Lombardi installed the T-formation, which Ralph Jones and Clark Shaughnessy had cooked up for the Chicago Bears in the 1930s, and which would soon infiltrate both the college and pro ranks like a virus. Using the novel scheme, St. Cecilia won thirty-six games in a row and six New Jersey state championships; Lombardi was promoted to head football, basketball, and baseball coach in 1942, and his basketball team won the state parochial school title three years later.

After eight years in Englewood, Lombardi returned to Fordham in 1947 as coach of the freshman football team, which in that era was an entity separate from the varsity squad. He once again installed the T, and again did well with it. The next year, varsity head coach Ed Danowski made Lombardi his offensive assistant.

That role lasted just a year. In 1949, he moved on again and became an assistant to Col. Earl (Red) Blaik at the U.S. Military Academy. (Another future Pro Football Hall of Fame coach, Sid Gillman, left as Lombardi arrived.) The Army football team, benefiting from war-time eligibility rules, had become the NCAA's pre-eminent college power in the 1940s, and was still among the nation's elite when Lombardi got to

ABOVE After college, Lombardi was hired at St. Cecilia High in Englewood, New Jersey. He coached three sports and taught three subjects.

West Point, New York. The Cadets were, in fact, in the midst of what would become a 27-game unbeaten streak. It didn't end until a humiliating defeat to Navy in the final game of the 1950 season.

Things went downhill from there. In 1951, the Academy was rocked by an academic cheating scandal. Ninety cadets were given administrative discharges, including fifty-one football players—one of them Blaik's son. Decimated, the Army team floundered for two seasons before rebounding to go 7-1-1 in 1953. But Lombardi was gaining valuable on-the-job training.

Red Blaik was a serious, disciplined but dignified leader who became a mentor to Lombardi. The younger coach borrowed directly in some cases—for example, his execution of crisp, 90-minute practices. More to the point, he seemed to adopt Blaik's views of commitment and chain of command. "The most important thing that ever happened to me in football was the opportunity to coach under Colonel Blaik," Lombardi told *Look* magazine in 1961. "Whatever success I have had must be attributed to 'the old man.' He molded my methods and my whole approach to the game. The unqualified superlative is precarious, but if there's a No. 1 coach of all time, in my opinion it is Colonel Blaik."

ABOVE The Army coaching staff in 1951. Head coach Red Blaik is wearing the windbreaker, and Lombardi is seated on Blaik's right.

T-FORMATION

When Lombardi ran the New York Giants' offense under head coach Jim Lee Howell, he favored three players in the backfield with the quarterback—as did most NFL teams. The two halfback/flankers were sort of hybrid runner-receivers, Frank Gifford epitomizing the position. They were expected to run between the tackles, but also had to be able to catch the ball downfield.

Notice that all of these play series are run from basically the same formation. The difference is the blocking schemes, which influence the direction of the play. Notice also the absence of a true tight end in these formations. The offense tended to feature a pair of split ends in addition to the men in the backfield. This setup spread defenses laterally, but didn't give Lombardi the off-tackle power he would come to rely upon later.

When he got to Green Bay in 1959, Lombardi would deploy a tight end, or Y end, along with one split end. And with his offense struggling during his first season there, he would scrap the four-man backfield and move rookie Boyd Dowler wide into a true flanker position.

He would, however, retain many of the offensive principles and blocking schemes of his Giants days, as evidenced by the sweep options diagrammed here. The inside belly play—a quick-hitting cutback run designed to take advantage of an aggressive defensive tackle—would remain one of his staples.

VI. GIANT OFFENSE
Split 'T'

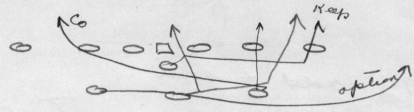

Belly Series

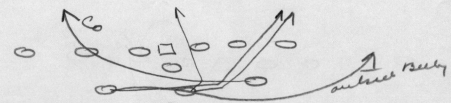

Full Back Buck Series

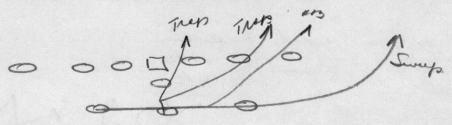

Sweep and Power series

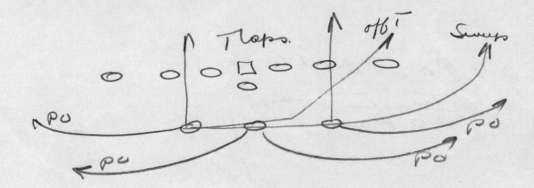

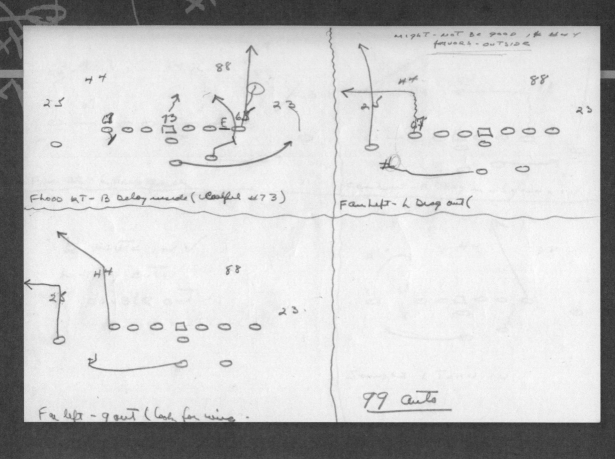

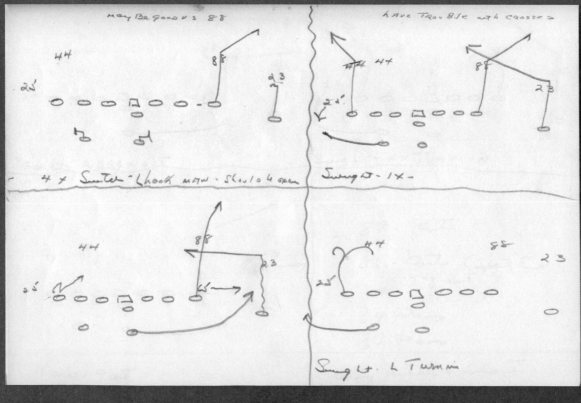

Stirring words by a coach who, nearly fifty years later, is considered by many to be the greatest of all time.

While coaching under Blaik, Lombardi harbored a quiet desire to return to Fordham as head coach. But the school dropped football after the 1954 season—to Lombardi's lasting disgust. By then he had moved in another direction, joining the pro football ranks with the New York Giants. Jim Lee Howell had been promoted to replace outgoing legend Steve Owen, and he made Lombardi his offensive assistant.

In a pattern that would be repeated throughout his NFL tenure, Lombardi's team showed marked improvement in his first year. The Giants had gone 3-9 in 1953, then climbed to 7-5 in 1954, their point total jumping from 179 to 293. They would not have a losing record during Lombardi's five seasons in New York.

The offensive mastermind from Brooklyn couldn't take all the credit for the turnaround, however. The Giants' chief defensive assistant was Tom Landry, an all-pro defensive back who became player-coach under Howell in 1954. Landry's 4-3-4 defense was one of the NFL's best, and he got his chance to be a head coach in 1960, taking over the fledgling Dallas Cowboys a year after Lombardi went to Green Bay. He would coach in Dallas through 1988 and win 270 games. (The intensely competitive Lombardi never could stomach losing to anyone, but during his years with the Packers, he got particularly wound up when his team was playing either the Giants or the Cowboys, and he beat them in some of Green Bay's most famous games.)

Lombardi's time in New York was happy, though. He was within cab fare to practically all of his friends and family, and a hero in the old neighborhood. Not yet burdened by the pressures of being a head coach, he was also a darling of the New York sports media, who often came to him for quotes or analysis.

On the field, Lombardi was momentarily in over his head. "Vinnie didn't understand our game when he first came here," star halfback Frank Gifford told *Time* magazine in 1962. "At

first, we players were showing him how it went. By the end of the year, though, he was showing us."

Lombardi tinkered with his T-formation and threw some wrinkles at the rest of the league. Every team in the NFL was running the T by 1954 (the Steelers were the last to junk the Single-Wing, in 1952), but most teams placed the flanker inside the end on what you could call the strong side. Lombardi set his flanker *outside*, and moved his strong-side end in close to the offensive tackle. In effect, it was a three-wide-receiver set. Soon this position would be called the tight end, a player that would prove pivotal to the Titletown-era Packers.

In fact, much of Lombardi's playbook was refined in New York. He ran the sweep and the halfback option and other signature plays of his Green Bay teams. Even the play terminology remained largely intact when he moved west. And already you could see Lombardi's big-picture thinking and attention to detail. His archives include personal scouting reports of the Colts' and Steelers' defensive units, drawn up during his days with the Giants. His Pittsburgh report, from 1955, offers commentary on each starter. Defensive tackle Dick Modzelewski would earn high praise over his fourteen NFL seasons, but Lombardi referred to him as "Modelewski" and called him "inexperienced." Linebacker John Reger, he said, "can be beat on swings." Dick Flanagan was an "excellent line backer."

By 1956, Gifford was the best all-around back in the league, a running and receiving threat who presaged the success of Paul Hornung in Green Bay. That year the Giants won six of their first seven games and became the first NFL team to deny Paul Brown's formidable Cleveland Browns a conference championship.

The Chicago Bears loomed in the 1956 NFL Championship Game, but it was no contest. New York quarterback Charlie Conerly (the original model for the Marlboro Man) completed seven of ten passes for 195 yards and a pair of touchdowns,

OPPOSITE Lombardi apparently drew up these "flash cards" specifically to game-plan the Baltimore Colts' defense in 1954. The right cornerback is future NFL coaching legend Don Shula.

23

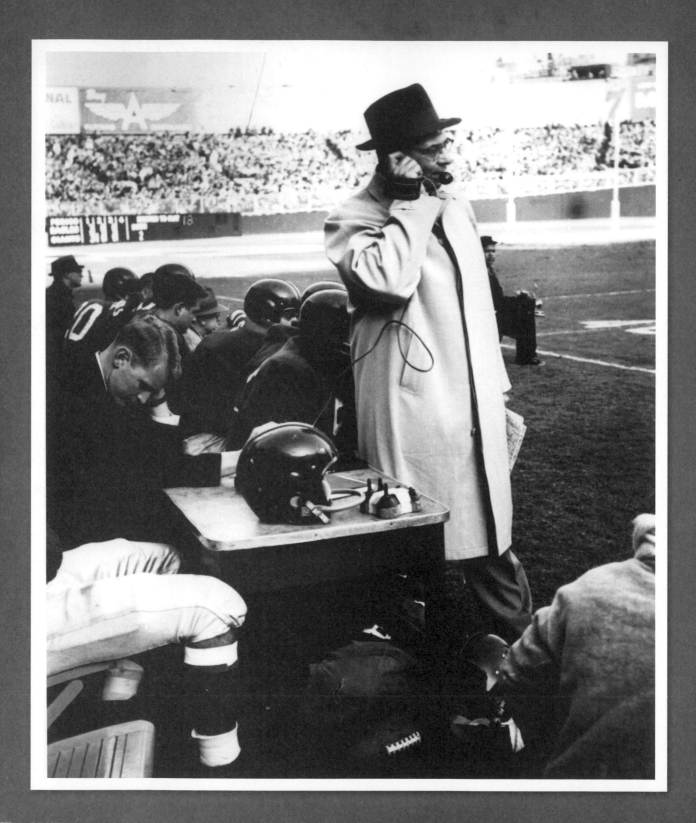

ABOVE Lombardi confers with another coach while on the Giants' sidelines.

Gifford had 161 yards from scrimmage, and the Giants breezed 47–7 on an icy field at their new home, Yankee Stadium. It was the team's first NFL title in eighteen years.

The Giants returned to the championship game in 1958, but lost to the Baltimore Colts 23–17 in what is now nonchalantly referred to as the greatest game ever played. A relatively huge TV audience tuned in to the game at Yankee Stadium and was treated to the first NFL postseason game ever to go into sudden-death overtime. The Colts prevailed when fullback Alan Ameche burst into the end zone for a touchdown 8:15 into the extra period.

It was Lombardi's last game in New York. During his five years with the team, he was linked to jobs at USC, Washington, Stanford, Air Force, and Pennsylvania, but nothing came of their interest. In 1959, however, a floundering NFL franchise recruited him to restore its standing as a league power. "When the Green Bay chance came, I knew it was time to make a move, if ever I was to make one," Lombardi told *Look*.

He signed a five-year contract to become the Packers head coach and general manager on February 4, 1959, and moved his family—wife Marie, son Vincent, and daughter Susan—away from the bustle of New York and into the deep snow of a Wisconsin winter, to a quiet town of 63,000 football-starved people.

ABOVE Lombardi gathers with some of his players after joining the Packers in 1959. Seated at center is quarterback Bart Starr.

BUILDING BLOCK 2

THE LOMBARDI SWEEP

At the height of Operation Desert Storm in February
1991, Ron Kramer was watching the news on television.
General Norman Schwarzkopf, chief of U.S. ground forces in
the Persian Gulf, was detailing an assault by his forces into
Iraq, using arrows and diagrams to graphically illustrate
the maneuvers. Kramer, who played tight end in Green Bay
from 1957 to 1964, squinted into his TV set. He had seen
those arrows before.

"I wrote a letter General Schwarzkopf," Kramer says.
"I sent 49 to him and told him he had plagiarized Vince. He
was at Army when Vince was there."

Schwarzkopf indeed played football at West Point, and
his time there overlapped with Lombardi's, when the latter
was an assistant under Army coach Red Blaik. The general
wrote back to Kramer, saying Lombardi had hit him harder
than anyone else at any time.

The 49 to which Kramer referred was a basic sweep
play: the 4 back through the 9 hole, which wasn't really
a hole at all but the far right flank of the offensive line.
If Vince Lombardi's offensive system were a monument
to football, the sweep would be its cornerstone. This one
play both symbolized the offense and made the totality
possible, and it became synonymous with the great Packers teams of the sixties. In fact, though other teams ran a

similar play, people soon called it the Lombardi Sweep or
the Packer Sweep.

It didn't begin in Green Bay, though. Lombardi acknowl-
edged that it went back to his playing days at Fordham. "I
was impressed, playing against the single-wing sweep, the
way those Pittsburgh teams of Jock Sutherland ran it," he told
editor George Flynn during an interview for the film series
Vince Lombardi's The Science and Art of Football (collected in the
two-volume set *Lombardi on Football*). "And I was impressed
afterward when I attended coaching clinics and the single
wing was discussed. . . . Today, our sweep has a lot of those
Sutherland qualities, the same guard-pulling technique, the
same ball carriers' cut-back feature."

Lombardi also noticed that the Los Angeles Rams were
running the sweep in the 1950s. He studied their film for
hours, and he installed the play in his playbook when he
became a Giants assistant in 1954. Later, Paul Hornung would

OPPOSITE Right guard Jerry Kramer leads halfback Paul Hornung around the right end on a classic sweep play. **ABOVE** Left guard Fuzzy Thurston gets his chance to convoy Hornung.

27

be the halfback who ran the sweep to perfection; in New York it was Frank Gifford. "Though neither had that blinding speed, they both were quick, intelligent runners who could 'control' their running so that they used their blockers and got every possible yard out of each play," Lombardi said.

When the new coach arrived in Green Bay in 1959, he quickly made it clear that the sweep would be the foundation of his offense. As former wide receiver Boyd Dowler remembers: "He told us from Day One, 'The sweep is what we'll sleep with. It will be our lead play from split backs'— which we called red formation. 'We have to make it work, and other things will work because of it.'"

Lombardi never abandoned the sweep during his nine seasons in Green Bay. Over the years, NFL defenses began to catch up with it a little, so he ran it with less regularity. But

it was there when he needed it. AFL teams hadn't seen the sweep nearly as much, so when the Packers faced the Chiefs in Super Bowl I, they ran fullback Jim Taylor on a sweep left and he scored from 14 yards out, breaking a 7–7 tie in the second quarter.

You'd think that teams would have figured out how to stop the play entirely. "Some people did every once in a while," Ron Kramer says. "But not often. The obvious reason is that we were probably mentally and physically in better shape than most people."

Despite its nearly mythic status, the sweep was a fairly simple play at its core. Or perhaps its simplicity is part of its legend. The offside back—if the play was going to the right, as it usually did, this would the back lined up behind the quarterback and to his left, the halfback—would follow not

ABOVE The sweep could go left as well as right. Here, Tom Moore follows his guards against the Cardinals in 1963.

only the other back, but both guards and the offside tackle, all of whom would swing around in a tight arc and form a convoy. The ball carrier would read their blocks and either take the play around the corner and outside, or cut upfield inside of a potential tackler.

Of all the players involved, it is the guards who are perhaps most strongly associated with the sweep. On most plays, then and now, they are anonymous brutes who engage in hand-to-hand grappling in the middle of the scrum, where no one but the most trained eye can see them or appreciate their efforts. They are, in fact, all but invisible to most fans.

The sweep liberated the guards, loosening the knot of players in the middle of the field and sending them out into the light, where they became mobile 250-pound tanks looking for something to blow up. Fuzzy Thurston and Jerry Kramer, then Gale Gillingham, and for shorter periods of time Forrest Gregg and Dan Grimm—all of them ran the sweep to perfection. It took tremendous conditioning, especially during an era when full-time offseason jobs made year-round cardiovascular work impossible.

"You see this?" Thurston asks. He's in his landmark Green Bay bar, Fuzzy's No. 63 (a reference to his uniform number), and he's pointing to an old framed photograph of a sweep in progress. He and Jerry Kramer are on the move and rumbling.

"Look at my eyes," Thurston says. Seen through his facemask, they are practically bulging out their sockets with some combination of anticipation, fury, and focus. "I'm about to knock some poor S.O.B. on his ass."

It wasn't just the guards, of course. Whichever back wasn't carrying the ball was expected to become a lead blocker, and the versatility of Lombardi's backs was part of what made his sweep so successful. Jim Taylor was a good runner at fullback, and halfback Paul Hornung, despite his movie-star appeal, was a tough blocker. After Hornung's abilities faded and Taylor jumped to the Saints, guys like Donny Anderson, Elijah Pitts, and Jim Grabowski ran the

ABOVE Thurston (63) and Kramer (64) formed one of the 1960s' best guard tandems. Thurston (bottom) was the class clown.

69 - odd + even.

69 Pass - l x R - wing trail

49 - odd + even.

49 - Pass ① HB
           ② QB

29 PO - odd + even

   alternate way.
29 PO Pass

347 -
347 Pass

THE SWEEP

The Lombardi Sweep was known as 49 to his players —the 4-back (or halfback) going through the 9-hole (or around the right edge). It could go to the left, too, in which case the halfback would block for the fullback, but the classic sweep sent Paul Hornung or another halfback around the right corner.

The 49 diagram at left illustrates the play against a straight 4-3 defense. It's rudimentary, but you can see four of the nine blocking assignments: The fullback charges off the right tackle's shoulder to drive the onside defensive end, the right tackle hunts down the middle linebacker, the tight end or Y end prevents the outside linebacker from getting inside, and the wing back or flanker simulates a pass play before zeroing in on the cornerback or safety to his side.

There is plenty you don't see in this diagram. The key, outside of the Y end's block, is the pulling action of the guards. Both drop off the line and arc around the right side, gaining steam to lead the halfback. The right guard swings outside the Y end's block and hits the first defender he sees, often the cornerback to that side. The left guard pulls directly down the line of scrimmage, rounding out his path after getting past the quarterback.

Meanwhile, the center blocks down on a defensive tackle, the split end or weakside end releases for the weakside safety, and the left tackle takes a deep pull to cut down any interference that may have filtered into the backfield.

sweep nearly as ably. "You've gotta have the right personnel for it," former quarterback Zeke Bratkowski says. "If you look at the game now, you can count on one hand the number of times a fullback carries in one year. In our game, Hornung and Taylor and all the different backs, those guys had to run and block, so there was no obvious tendency."

Assuming the play was to the halfback, the fullback was expected to make a beeline to the outside of the onside tackle and hit the first guy he encountered to deny penetration. "The fullback drives right at the first man that shows; I mean, the first defensive man the fullback sees," Lombardi advised. This would be the defensive end or the middle linebacker; the fullback was, in essence, protecting those lanes the guards would run within.

The offensive tackles were nearly as important as the guards in the sweep. The onside tackle would either block the man directly over him or, if there was none, hunt for the middle linebacker. "Whether you got him or not depended on who he was," says Forrest Gregg, who most often played right tackle for the Packers. "Dick Butkus wasn't easy to get."

The offside tackle? He had to pull out and get on the move, just like the guards. "He'd pick up anything that was filtering through the line that had a chance to make a play on the running back," Gregg says. "Or sometimes the guard in front of him would get knocked down, and he'd have to get out and lead."

But of all the blocks on the field, the most important for the sweep may have been the tight end's. He had an option block on his opponent, usually an outside linebacker. If the linebacker took an inside track, the tight end would seal him off from the outside and drive him parallel to the line of scrimmage. If the linebacker went outside, the tight end would take him that way. "We tell the Y end that under no circumstances should he allow penetration to the inside," the coach was quoted as saying in *Lombardi on Football*, the two-volume set published posthumously in 1973. "We do not care how much penetration the defensive man gets to the outside."

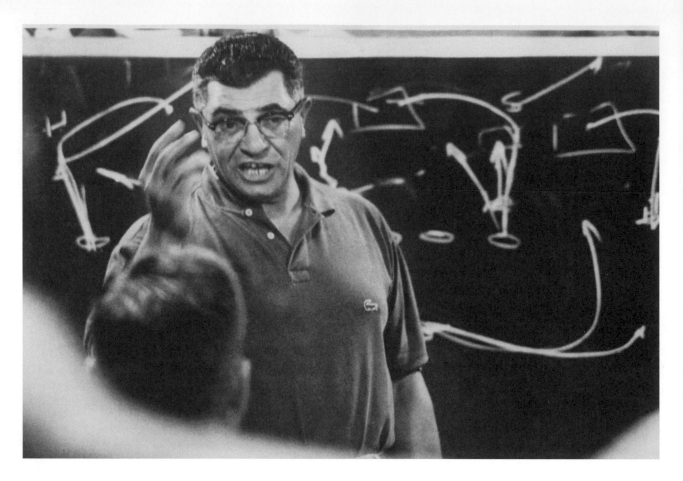

The ball carrier would read the tight end's block and make his decision, inside or out. It was all pretty straightforward, really. And yet the sweep powered the Green Bay scoring machine and vexed NFL defenses for a decade. Other teams weren't able to duplicate the play with any regularity.

"They didn't have Fuzzy and Jerry," Thurston says with a mischievous smile. "Plus, you've got to have great tackles, great tight ends, great blocking backs. If you have one weakness, it won't go. That's why they don't do it anymore. You had to get eleven guys not to make a mistake."

Supposedly, that's one of the things Lombardi loved about the sweep. It epitomized the concept of team play.

The Packer Sweep dominated not with trickery, but through precision. Normally Lombardi had his offensive linemen line up 30 to 36 inches apart; on this play he preferred wider splits, 40 inches. This spread the front wall laterally. The tight end was instructed to position himself exactly nine feet outside the offensive tackle. *Exactly* nine feet. The route taken by the pulling guards had to be equally precise. "That was the hardest part for me, getting those poles down," says Gillingham, who had never played guard before joining the Packers as a rookie in 1966. "They wanted you at the exact depth every time. If you were lead guard, they wanted you 4½ yards deep. You had to clear that fullback, you know? That deep pull from the left side was hard."

Perfection didn't come easy. Lombardi began teaching the sweep by drilling it at the chalkboard, starting from scratch every year. Then came mind-numbing repetition on the practice field, the same basic play re-run endlessly. It was not uncommon for Lombardi to order the sweep run

ABOVE The sweep, like all of Lombardi's plays, began as an endlessly diagrammed play on a meeting-room chalkboard.

ABOVE The coach uses a blocking dummy for a chance to get off his feet at practice.

exclusively for 30 minutes straight in practice. "There's nothing spectacular about it," he said. "It's just a yard gainer, and I've diagrammed it so many times and coached it so much and watched it evolve so often since I first put it in with the Giants eight years ago that I think I see it in my sleep."

So did his players. Thurston says the Packers probably ran it 50 to 60 times in practice every week. And that was late-season workouts, too, not just training camp. Little wonder that fifty years after the fact, Ron Kramer can walk you through the Lombardi Sweep over the phone, describing not only his role but all of his offensive teammates' against a standard 4-3 defensive scheme. "I can tell you any defense they might play, and how you block it," he adds.

Lombardi felt one of the great advantages of the sweep was that he could run it against an odd defense—with a defender stationed directly over the center's nose—or an even one. Likewise, he could run it against an over formation (with the defensive linemen overshifted to the strong side and the linebackers shifted weak) or an under formation (with the relative positions reversed).

Each player internalized as many as twenty options on the play, contingencies for various reactions by the defense. And if a defense presented a particular challenge to the sweep—either because of a strategic ploy or the extraordinary skills of an individual player—Lombardi and his play-caller, Bart Starr, usually had an answer.

The classic parry was the influence play or, more colorfully, the sucker play. A major threat to the sweep was an athletic offside defensive tackle. Say the sweep was going to the right. The left guard would drop-step and pull around the right end, leaving the man lined up in front of him, the offside defensive tackle, with no one in his face. Usually it wasn't a big deal, because most defensive tackles weren't quick enough to chase down the play from behind, and they often got picked off by the trailing left offensive tackle. But someone like the Rams' Merlin Olsen or Detroit's Alex Karras, if they were anticipating the sweep, could shoot the gap and blow up the halfback before he was safely behind

his convoy. In such a case, the Packers might call a sucker play. They'd begin to sweep, every offensive player selling the notion. But the fullback, after taking a jab step to the right, would go against the flow of the play, take a handoff and head straight for the hole vacated by the left guard and his foil, the defensive tackle.

"That's why we call it a sucker play," the coach noted in *Lombardi on Football*. "We fake sweep, suck him into following the halfback, and then run the fullback right into his area. After this has happened to that tackle, he will be a little leery about chasing the sweep so quickly."

The most memorable use of the sucker play came against Dallas in the 1967 NFL Championship Game, better known as the Ice Bowl. Cowboys defensive tackle Bob Lilly had been destroying the sweep for much of the day. Starr waited all afternoon, then finally called the influence play with less than a minute left and the ball on the Dallas 11-yard line. It worked to perfection, and fullback Chuck Mercein ran through Lilly's hole for eight yards, setting up the decisive touchdown.

The sucker play wasn't the Packers' only recourse, either. They also had the long trap, the weak-side sweep, and the halfback option, among others. The long trap did to aggressive defensive ends what the sucker play did to defensive tackles. Onside defensive ends would sometimes thwart the sweep by making a hard, deep outside move to get in the guards' way and force the play deep. The long trap would use his decisiveness against him. The pulling offside guard would seal the defensive end from the inside, and the ball carrier, rather than continuing outside, would cut in front of the guard's block.

In the Western Conference Championship Game against the Rams in 1967, the Packers victimized Deacon Jones, one of the best defensive ends in history, with the long trap. Halfback Travis Williams made his cut and raced 46 yards for Green Bay's first touchdown.

Lombardi would also sweep to the opposite direction. It was the weak-side sweep, where the halfback would lead

OPPOSITE Nearly as important as execution of the sweep was the decision on when to use it, and that fell to Bart Starr.

ABOVE When defenses keyed on the sweep, Lombardi had surprises up his sleeve—like this halfback option pass by Hornung.

the way around the weak side, generally the left side, and the fullback would follow him with the ball. This play was usually a reaction to rotation by the safeties. Often defenses would try to get a jump on the basic sweep by rotating their safeties toward the strong side: The strong safety would creep down close to the tight end, ready to pounce into the backfield, and the free safety would compensate by drifting into the middle of the field. The weak-side sweep would take advantage of the imbalance and run away from rotation of the safeties. The key was the offside end, who would take a nine-foot split outside the left offensive tackle and become a de facto tight end. The Packers ran this version of the sweep against the Chiefs in Super Bowl I, and Max McGee famously took out three potential tacklers like dominoes—the weak side linebacker, the right defensive end, and the middle linebacker. Taylor followed his guards and found the end zone.

Finally, the halfback option pass was the ultimate trump card on sweep plays. Like Frank Gifford before him, Paul Hornung could throw the ball with accuracy. Occasionally a defense would read the sweep and charge hard to contain it, only to watch Hornung pull back and throw to his tight end, who had held his block on the outside linebacker for three long seconds before releasing into a flat route.

With its many counter-counters, the sweep became a system unto itself. If a defense didn't honor it, Lombardi and Starr would sweep down the field. If the defenders committed to stopping it, the Packers would turn that, too, to their advantage. "It's the players, the play, the time spent practicing, and matching the players to the position," Forrest Gregg says.

Sounds easy. Looked easy, too, thanks to massive effort. But no one ever ran the sweep like Lombardi's Packers. Never has a single play defined a football team so clearly or played such a central role in its success.

ABOVE Thurston (63) and fullback Jim Taylor (31) pave the way for Hornung against the Browns on a muddy field.

37

3

RUN TO WIN
LOMBARDI'S GROUND GAME

Vince Lombardi was a lot of things—a motivator, an organizer, a teacher, occasionally a visionary, and yes, often a tyrant—but no one ever accused him of being a trickster. When you played the Green Bay Packers in the 1960s, you didn't do much guessing about the game plan. They were going to run the ball, and then run it some more. There were many variations and options within that running, but Lombardi's basic mode of attack was no secret.

"Some people said, 'If they give you the hitch [route] on first down, take it,'" former wide receiver Boyd Dowler reflects. "He didn't think that way. He'd rather run the ball on first down and make five yards than throw for five yards. It sounds stupid, but he believed the running game established superiority and toughness. You might be gaining seven or eight yards on that same play later in the game."

Not that Lombardi didn't incorporate deep passes and gadget plays in his offense. But it was all predicated on a strong, physical running game that forced defenses to over-compensate and thereby set them up for surprise strikes.

Lombardi had a practical respect for the run. He was an offensive lineman at Fordham in the 1930s, when running was just about all anyone did, and he believed it won football games even thirty years later. But his devotion to the ground game went beyond utility. He admired the teamwork necessary to turn a handoff into a yard gainer. "What it comes down to is that to have a good running game, you have to like to run as a coach," Lombardi said, as quoted by Vince Jr. in *The Essential Vince Lombardi*. "You have to derive more creative satisfaction from the planning and the polishing of the coordination of seven or eight men rather than two or three."

Really, it was more like eleven men. Lombardi didn't imagine his wide receivers would deliver crushing blocks on runs, but he expected them at least to get in the way of a defensive back, and sometimes to crack back on a linebacker. And his quarterback, usually Bart Starr, had to know which running plays to call, and to set up play-action passes by using the same handoff techniques consistently.

Many of Lombardi's run plays came from a split-backs set, or in his terms, Red formation. His primary backs, Jim Taylor and Paul Hornung, had noticeably different strengths; Taylor was bigger and stronger, Hornung quicker and more

---

OPPOSITE When the yardage got tough, Jim Taylor got going. Here he runs against the Steelers. **ABOVE** Players say Lombardi would rather run for five yards than pass for five.

39

versatile. But in terms of their responsibilities, they were nearly interchangeable—both ran, both blocked, and opponents never knew which one would be leading the other on a given play.

That system seems like a relic now. As offenses came to rely more on timing and quickness over the last thirty years, coaches decided it took too long for the ball carrier to come across the center-quarterback plane and get to the hole from split backs. So most current NFL offenses use either a single-back set, or offset backs with the halfback directly behind the quarterback and a bruising fullback a little closer to the line, almost an H-back position. There's no longer any question who will get the ball. "There's still a lot of merit to split backs, but right now I don't see a lot of people utilizing them," says Starr's primary backup, Zeke Bratkowski, who spent some twenty-five years in coaching. "But they should. There are some plays there they could do some real good things with."

By the time he got to Green Bay, Lombardi already had a clear sense of how to establish a run game. *The Essential Vince Lombardi* includes these principles, from notes the coach made to himself:

- Know strongest blockers.
- Run at tired or dazed defenders.
- Run at weak links on plays of importance.
- Don't depend on making ten yards consistently.
- The best play is always the best call on first down—get as much yardage.
- Second and short—still best possible situation.
- Stick to running game if good; don't switch for the sake of switching.
- Inside and outside.
- Don't be patterned according to down or position.

His bread and butter was, of course, the power sweep, a.k.a. the Packer Sweep, a.k.a. the Lombardi Sweep. When it was humming, everything else in the playbook flowed from it. But Lombardi had a lot more in his arsenal, much of it unadorned.

One proven tactic was running off-tackle. "The off-tackle play is one of the oldest plays in football, reminiscent of the days of the single wing, but it remains a fundamental play that teams must be able to execute and execute well," he said in the *Lombardi on Football* compilation.

On this simple maneuver, the halfback cuts through the hole between the offensive tackle and the tight end. The tackle blocks the defensive end, the tight end either doubles on the D-end or goes searching for the middle linebacker, the offside guard (that is, the one on the far side of the play) pulls into the running lane and hammers the outside linebacker, and the fullback takes care of the cornerback on the side of the play.

"The quarterback opens up to the left halfback and makes the hand-off almost directly behind the center, being very careful not to force the left halfback too far from the line of scrimmage," Lombardi instructed. "The left halfback comes across parallel to the line of scrimmage and drives through the hole."

The veer play was another building block. Few plays looked simpler. In fact, to the untrained eye, the veer must have resembled a massive freeway pileup. But it required multiple diagnoses and reactions from at least four offensive lineman, and a quick decision by the fullback, who carried the ball on this play. "The veer play, which is really a take-off on the dive play, is a favorite of mine because it gives the back the opportunity to read the block of his guard and center and to be able to run to daylight," the coach said in *Lombardi on Football*.

Lombardi felt the veer was particularly effective against an odd defensive front, with a man stationed directly over the center (as was often the case in the 1960s). The blocking was much the same whether against odd or even, though the center's ability to push the nose tackle one way or the other became paramount against an odd defense. "That's why we like this play; we don't care what kind of defenses they're going to throw at us, we're going to run this veer play on them!" Lombardi crowed.

OPPOSITE Lombardi didn't want his offense to look like "typewriter keys" getting off the line on running plays.

The offensive linemen liked the veer, as well as other plays up the middle, because they were macho tests of strength and aggressiveness. "When everything went to hell and we started having trouble, we all started screaming for the 0 and 1 hole, which was straight ahead," former guard Gale Gillingham says. "Get things back in control, and we were going to the sidelines. That was Lombardi's main thing, drive blocking. He wanted people moved."

Fuzzy Thurston, the one-time guard and long-time tavern owner in Green Bay, liked the up-the-middle plays, too, and is still happy to demonstrate the switch blocks he and center Jim Ringo would execute—Ringo blocking down on the defensive tackle in Thurston's face, Fuzzy in turn going after the middle linebacker. "Ringo was so quick, I'd step there and he was gone," Thurston says with admiration.

But the play that made Jim Taylor great may have been the weakside fullback slant—36 or 37 in the playbook—another simple creation that defenses never truly found a way to stop. "Taylor has great balance and he can cut quickly, and our best play is a simple fullback slant," Lombardi told *Sports Illustrated* photographer Robert Riger, as recounted in the 1961 *Green Bay Packers Yearbook*. "He can run it over tackle and if that hole closes he can come back over the center or he can swing wide outside. Three plays right there off one because Taylor makes them work."

Again, you see Lombardi's love for reading blocks—and for creating options on the blocks themselves. On the fullback slant, the split end would go after either the cornerback or the safety to his side, depending on which one forced the play. Meanwhile, the onside offensive tackle and the halfback would work as a team to wrap up the defensive end and outside linebacker to their side, and the onside guard and the center would do the same with a defensive tackle and the middle linebacker. Every defensive move had a prescribed counter-attack.

When a defense keyed on the slant, either pursuing strongly or taking direct angles across the line of scrimmage, Lombardi and Starr would turn to the fullback veer, which

TOSS AND DIP

Here are some basic runs to the left, three of them out of a power-left formation and one with split backs. Lombardi was never shy about getting his guards on the run, as these plays illustrate. The left guard pulls out in front on all four plays, and the right guard gets into the act on the 28 play.

The coach, in fact, asked a lot of all his blockers. In most of the plays shown here, the left tackle has to get into the "second level" to hunt for a linebacker, and it's up to the fullback to seal the right defensive end—who probably outweighed him by a good 30 pounds. The split end, meanwhile, is responsible for an outside linebacker; the Green Bay receivers had to be more than pass catchers.

Lombardi had plays that worked better against odd or even defensive fronts, and quarterback Bart Starr was expected to audible out of bad calls. These plays are illustrated against an even front (the center is uncovered), but were believed to work against either.

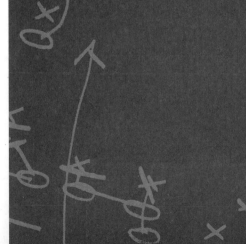

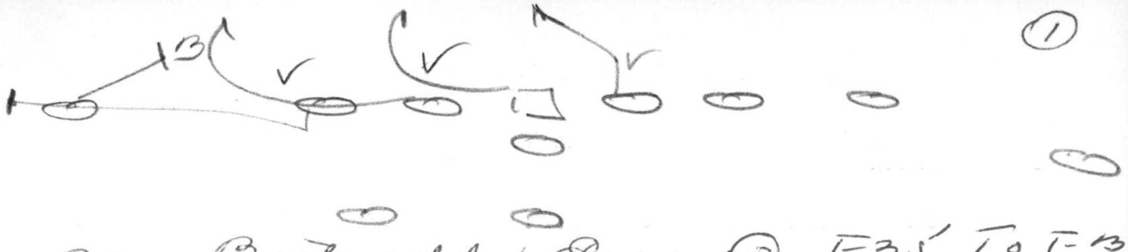

49 PO - Both odd + Even ② F35 TO T-13
                                odd + Even

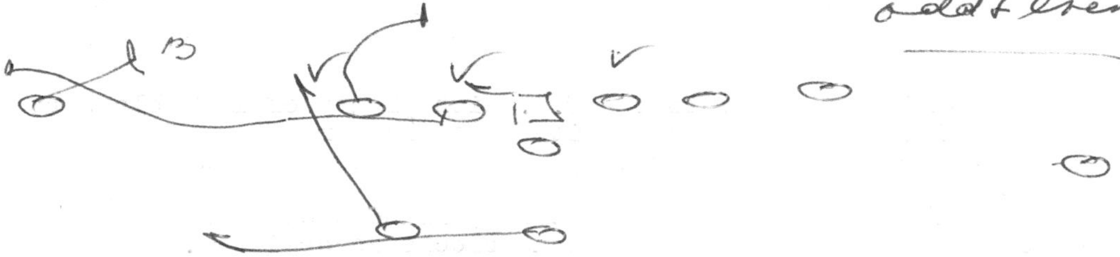

38 Toss - odd + Even

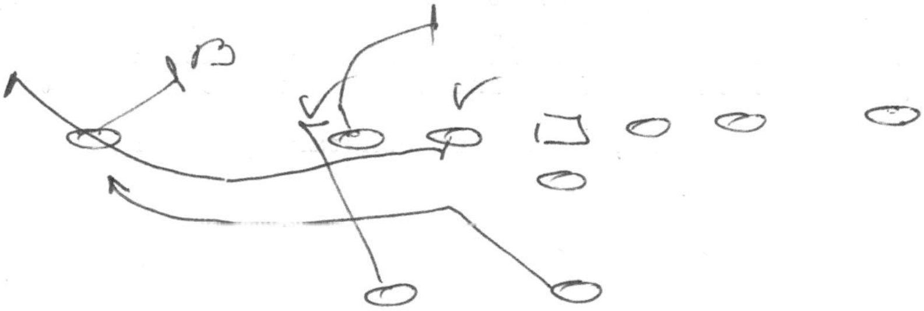

38 Dip - odd + Even

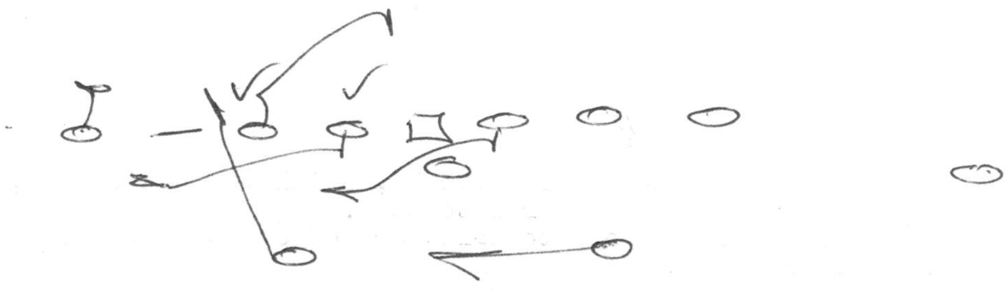

28 - odd + Even

① fake 38 Pass - L Slant
② 49 PO Pass

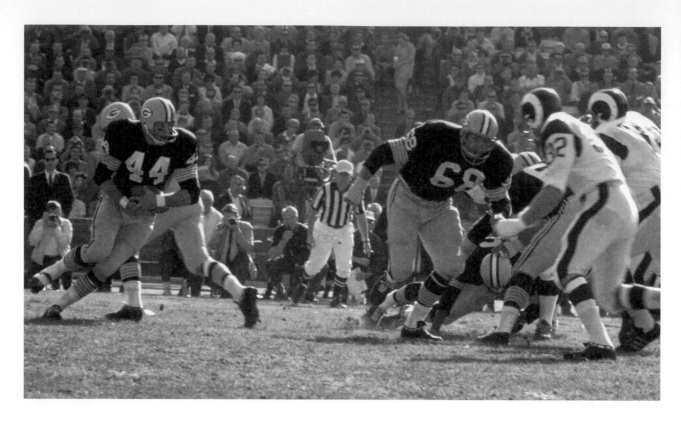

started like the slant but then cut back inside. Or they would simply run the ball up the middle. That's what they did when the Giants loaded up against the fullback slant in the 1961 NFL Championship Game. New York overshifted to the weak side and left middle linebacker Sam Huff over a guard. So the Packers repeatedly ran straight at Huff, relying on Taylor to read his blocks. He broke one inside run for 45 yards.

There were other indispensable plays in Lombardi's files, like the quick trap, the inside belly play, and the fullback toss weak. Lombardi favored the trap when Starr was getting undue pressure up the middle on pass plays, or when the middle linebacker vacated his post. The center would block one defensive tackle, and the offside guard would trap the other, leaving a hole for the halfback to burst into. Lombardi claimed the Packers scored sixteen touchdowns in one season on the goal-line version of the quick trap.

Lombardi liked the fullback toss weak when the offside defensive end was playing tight and the free safety was

favoring the strong side of the alignment. The inside belly play—a quick-hitting misdirection that involved a fake to the fullback running right, then a handoff to the halfback, who ran between left guard and tackle—came in handy against defensive tackles who were doggedly following the pull of the guards.

And while Bart Starr was never once confused with contemporary scramblers like Fran Tarkenton or Jack Kemp, Lombardi installed running plays for his quarterback. He was not averse to the quarterback sneak, the quarterback draw, the roll-out option pass or the bootleg.

"In today's game it is not considered good form to have the quarterback run very much," he says in *Lombardi on Football*, "but as long as you have a quarterback who has the potential for a long gain it's a very, very valuable weapon for the offense, and must make the defense play a little bit more honest."

Halfback, fullback or quarterback, inside or outside, left or right, Lombardi's individual running plays were fairly

ABOVE Gillingham (68) clears a path for running back Donny Anderson (44) against the Los Angeles Rams.

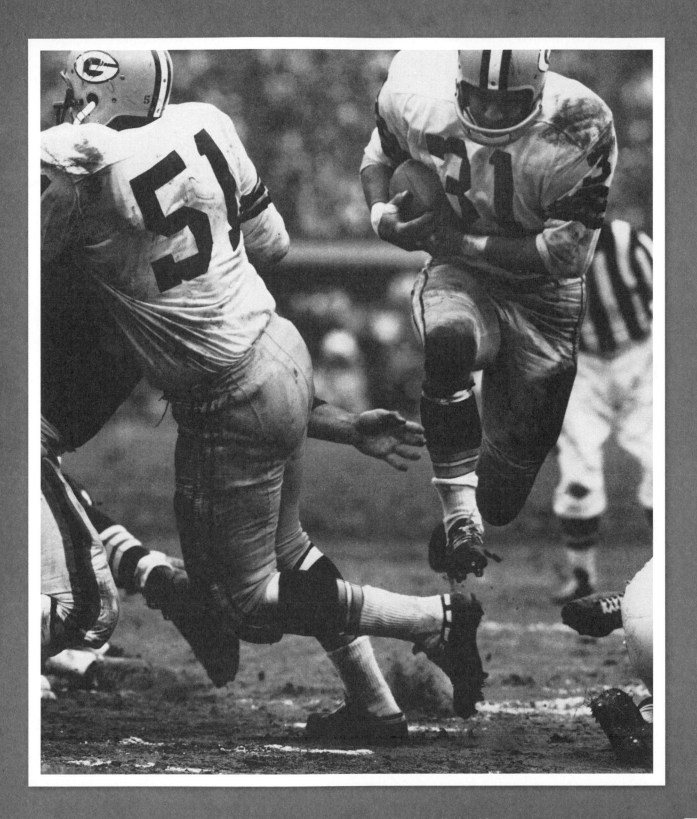

ABOVE Center Jim Ringo (51) springs Taylor in a 1961 game against the Browns at Cleveland's Municipal Stadium.

43 Double Pinch – L. End out.
Backs right

BACKS

BACKS

BACKS

DOUBLE PINCH

The pinch block was a specific type of double-team block that Lombardi liked. (He also called it the post-drive block.) It was a power technique most often used in short-yardage situations.

On a pinch block, the "post man" had to take a short step and plant his head directly in the sternum of a charging defensive lineman. Almost simultaneously, the "pinch man" next to him would down block from the side. Their main objective was to prevent the defender from splitting the two of them and penetrating.

The 43 Double Pinch play (4 back through the 3 hole) incorporated two pinch blocks and was certainly a short-yardage play; look how the fullback is positioned right behind the tight end, in sort of an H-back role. The variations at top and bottom are against an odd front (nose tackle over the center), and are almost identical. The middle variation is against an even front.

In both, the center and right guard work in tandem to neutralize a defensive lineman, either a nose tackle or a defensive tackle. On the other side of the gap, the right tackle and the tight end do the same with a defensive end. The fullback comes behind the right pinch to stop a linebacker, and the halfback takes the ball and darts through the space between the two pinch blocks.

standard fare on paper. On the field they became rugged ballets, the perfectly choreographed movements of eleven determined men.

In 1967, the Packers fell to Los Angeles in the regular season when the Rams blocked a punt and scored with less than minute remaining. Before their rematch in the Western Conference playoff game, Lombardi gave his players a theme for the week: Run to Win. He lifted it straight from the epistles of St. Paul: "Do you know that all who run in a race, all indeed run—but only one receives the prize. So run to win."

Lombardi wasn't being ironic or glib or intentionally hyperbolic, certainly not blasphemous. Faith in the Catholic God was perhaps his strongest passion. But a strong ground game was never far behind.

ABOVE Bart Starr (15) wasn't exactly nimble, but the Packers quarterbacks were expected to run when the situation called for it.

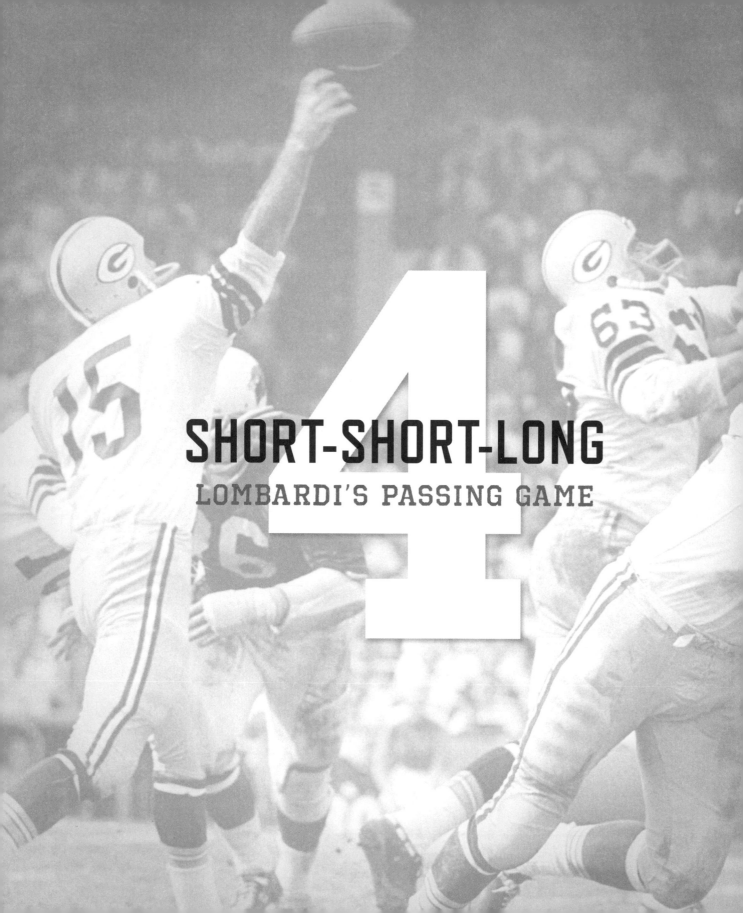

SHORT-SHORT-LONG
LOMBARDI'S PASSING GAME

Part of the reason the American Football League became
a legitimate rival to the NFL in the 1960s was the excitement
it generated in the passing game. Coaches like Sid Gillman
in San Diego and Al Davis in Oakland pushed the field both
horizontally and vertically, and several of their brethren
were happy to see their quarterbacks throw the ball forty
times a game.

Back in the NFL, the most dominant offense in the league
had a passing game designed not to exhaust or dizzy a defense, but to clinically exploit its shortcomings. In *Lombardi
on Football*, the famed coach confidently picks apart every
type of pass coverage a defense might throw at you. Man-
to-man defense, he said, put a great deal of pressure on the
cornerbacks and strong safety who had no help, and could
be exploited with post patterns. Zone defense, on the other
hand, could be hurt by the short passing game, with the
quarterback throwing underneath the linebackers or between
the cornerbacks and safeties. Combination defense, or double
coverage, left a defense vulnerable to flares by the fullback or
screens to the halfback. And against a "free-safety defense,"
Lombardi would send both backs out of the backfield, drawing the free safety to the sideline and opening up the middle
for the split end.

It didn't leave much hope for a defense, did it?

But Lombardi wasn't kidding himself. He knew that to
attack a defense as he suggested, his offensive players had
to be precisely coordinated and ruthlessly drilled. "Our
receivers and our backs must all be able to read their keys
on every pass play," *Lombardi on Football* tells us. "The Y
end usually keys the middle linebacker and the strong-side
safety. The flanker usually keys the strong-side linebacker,
the strong-side safety, and the strong-side halfback. The
split end keys the linebacker on his side, the weak-side
safety, and the cornerback playing over him. The backs
key the linebackers. On the snap of the ball the quarterback, depending on the play called, will key two or more
of these defenders."

A prison guard should carry around so many keys.

While the receivers had to read the coverage on every pass
play, Lombardi and his quarterback, Bart Starr, were thinking
further ahead. Both were obsessed with analyzing a defense's
tendencies and exploiting them whenever possible.

OPPOSITE Bart Starr throws against the St. Louis Cardinals in 1963. He led the NFL in passing yards in three seasons. **ABOVE** Lombardi didn't like to rely
heavily on pass plays, but nonetheless expected them to be executed perfectly.

49

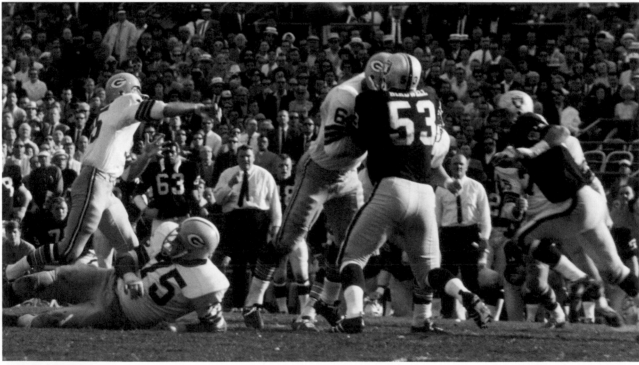

ABOVE Boyd Dowler grabs a touchdown pass in the 1966 NFL title game (top). Starr passes against the Raiders in Super Bowl II (bottom).

"If you go back and research all the films, I think you'll find we threw on first and second down often against Dallas," former flanker Carroll Dale says, offering an example. "It was simply because the Flex defense had two [defensive linemen] on the line, and two off. Coach Lombardi said it was a good run defense, but not a pass-rush defense. So we threw primarily on first down because we knew Dallas wouldn't be coming hard after the quarterback."

In the 1966 NFL Championship Game, the Packers took advantage of another of the Cowboys' habits. Starr knew that middle linebacker Lee Roy Jordan was good at getting into the flat and covering backs. So he called Flood Left X Delay and got Jordan to chase fullback Jim Taylor; split end Boyd Dowler blocked an outside linebacker briefly, then ran a crossing route and hauled in a 16-yard touchdown pass from Starr.

Lombardi tended to be conservative in crafting his passing game, but not timid. He was simply reacting to what the defense offered. "If they'd overload the line, we would throw every down if we had to," Dale says. "He was not stubborn, in that if you had seven people trying to beat eight, he would change the plan very quickly."

Often, opponents *would* try to stack the line. That's because the Green Bay running attack was so formidable. After a few eight-yard gains on the sweep, the defenders would usually start to creep into the box. That's when Starr and his offensive linemen would get the linebackers to charge by faking a handoff, then throw to a receiver in the open short zone. "Our play-action was always good, because of the fact we ran so well and Bart called it at the right time," Dowler says.

"We use this kind of play, naturally, in a running situation," Lombardi told Flynn. "We fake run when the whole defense expects run. . . . The easiest thing really to defend against is the pass in a passing situation. Second and long, third and long—that's easy. The most difficult thing to defend against is a pass in a running situation."

A classic display of Green Bay play-action came against the Raiders in the third quarter of Super Bowl II. It was third-and-1 at the Packers' 40-yard line. Starr faked a fullback run into the line, dropped back and found Max McGee loping behind safety Rodger Bird. The 35-yard gain helped set up a touchdown, and the Pack went on to win 33–14.

Lombardi liked to throw deep when it was unexpected. "If we threw on first down, we were going downfield," Dowler says. "We were trying for 20 yards, 15 yards, a touchdown." Even better was second-and-short. This is, in fact, the safest spot for a bomb. The defense has to honor the run in an ostensible short-yardage situation. And if you throw incomplete, you still have a good chance of picking up the first down on third-and-short.

"I suppose one of the marks that I will leave behind in this football game is the long pass to the free end on second and one for a touchdown," Starr says in *The Packer Legend*. "That was the timing I learned from Vince Lombardi. He would go along in a game, as he often said, hitting at their strength, but at just the right moment, he would call for an off-beat play which would completely take the other team by surprise."

Passes could set up other passes, too. That was just another way of fooling a defense by doing the unexpected. In a big early-season game against the Colts in 1966, Starr called a hitch-and-go to Dowler on third-and-5. He faked a short throw, then lofted to his tall receiver after he cut upfield. The play went for 25 yards and helped set up a clinching touchdown.

As with the running game, there were certain pass plays that became staples of the Green Bay scheme. One of them was Fullback Wide X & Y Wing Trail, which is about as wordy as Lombardi's terminology got. The coach's instructions on the play, drawn from *Lombardi on Football*, give of an indication of the execution he demanded:

"The split end splits to 7 yards. He's the first-named receiver and he goes deep, running almost a split between the weak-side halfback and the safety. His object is to occupy both of them, to pull both of them out of the area so that the Y end may come open.

"The Y end goes 3 to 4 yards downfield with an inside release on the strong-side linebacker, and runs an over pattern, crossing over to the other side of the field. He may go either underneath or behind the middle linebacker, but deepening his route so that in the area beyond his offensive tackle he should be 8 to 10 yards deep. The Y end will usually come open immediately after he passes the middle linebacker. If he has not come open then he will come open very late way across the field.

"The wingback splits 10 to 15 yards. He proceeds straight upfield approximately 15 yards and then runs a trail pattern, running directly across the field parallel to the line of scrimmage."

Meanwhile, the fullback runs a flat route, trying to pull the strongside linebacker with him, and the halfback, assuming there is no blitz, flares to the left and hopes that the weakside linebacker follows. The beauty of X & Y Wing Trail, like many of Lombardi's passes, is that the ball could wind up going to any receiver. "There was never a go-to receiver," Dowler says. "He didn't say, 'This is our No. 1 guy.' You had to be alert. I didn't know the ball was coming to me—unless I saw a certain defense, then I knew for certain."

In the aforementioned '66 championship game, Starr called Fullback Wide X & Y Wing Trail on third-and-19 at the Dallas 28-yard line, with a little more than five minutes left in the game. Taylor dragged the middle linebacker to the strong side, halfback Elijah Pitts picked up a blitz, and split end Max McGee was the open receiver. He faked the cornerback on a post route, then cut back to the corner and wound up with a 28-yard touchdown pass from Starr.

Combination patterns were also usually on the short list of plays. Today they might call them pick plays. Two receivers would cross the center of the field in close proximity; if the defensive backs were in man coverage, they'd have a hard time fighting through the traffic.

"Boyd Dowler and I did that well together," former tight end Ron Kramer says. "Boyd was 6'5", 224. I was 6'3", 234.

23 TRAP PASS

Judging by the 4-4 defensive alignment and the offensive formation featuring three backs and no flanker in the 23 Trap series, these plays would seem to be either remnants from Lombardi's Giants days or short-yardage change-of-pace passes—or both.

The main difference on the two 23 Trap Pass plays is the routes of the left and right ends. On the first, the left end runs a deeper post route while the right end comes back on a hook. On the second, the roles are fairly reversed—the left end crosses short while the right end runs a deep out or flag route.

Lombardi calls for a flanker on 39 Dip Pass, and this player and the left both take their routes toward the sidelines. Meanwhile, note the action of the right end and fullback. Their routes cross not once but twice as the fullback pulls a double move. This sort of "combination pattern" was designed to get cover men picked off in traffic.

23 Trap Pass — Roop Right

Gud

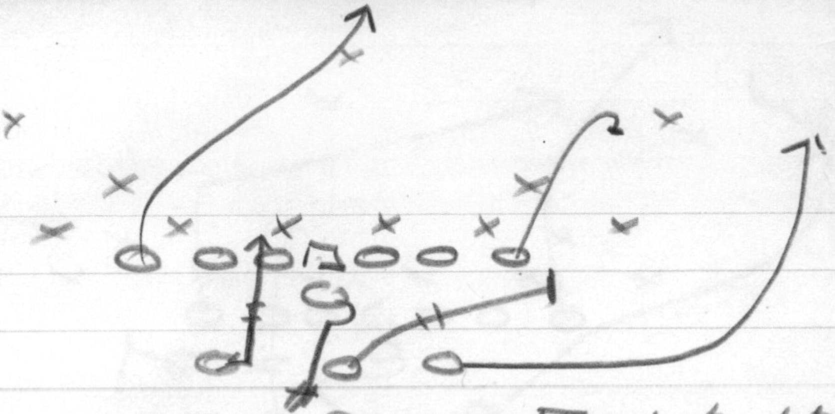

23 Trap Pass — Optional Right

Gud

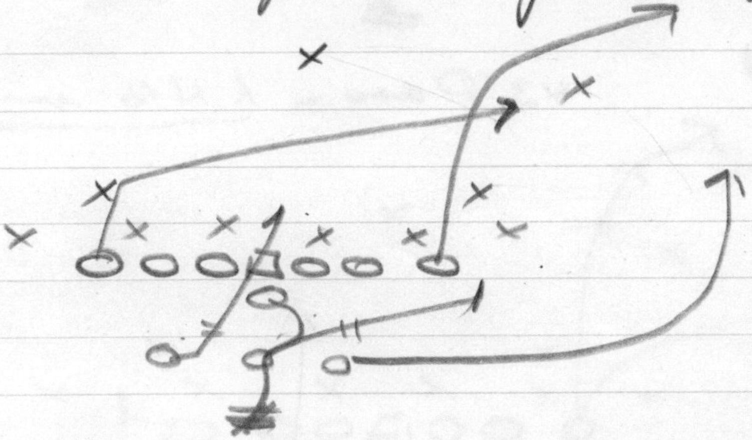

39 Dip Pass — Rain Bow Out

Tak

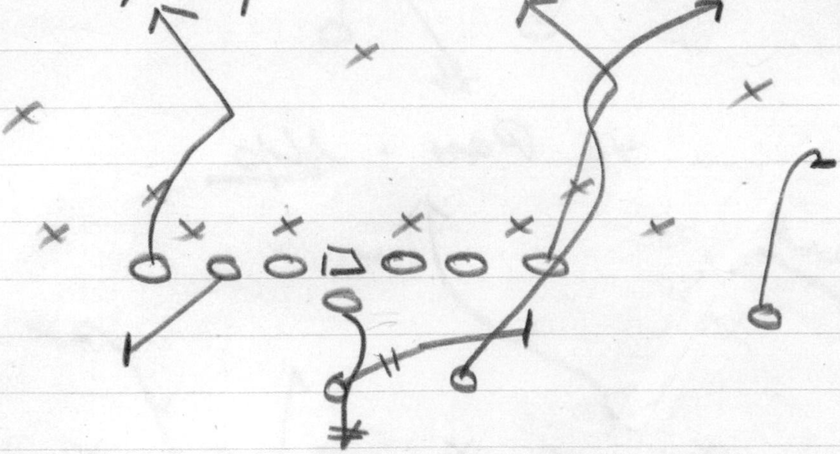

43 Pass - Either

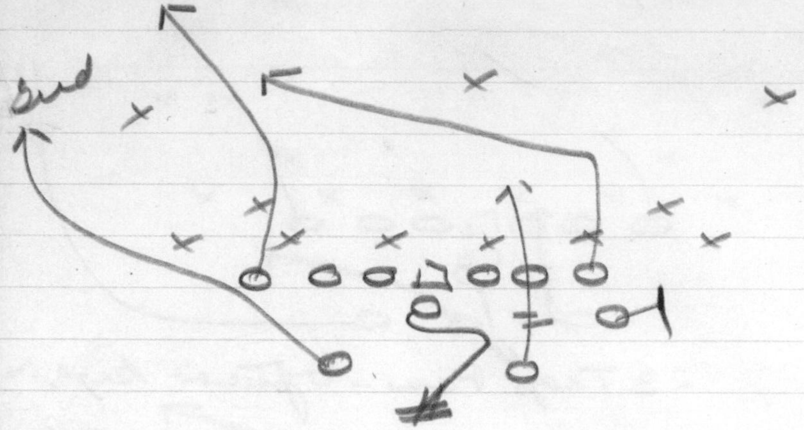

43 Pass - L H B in flat

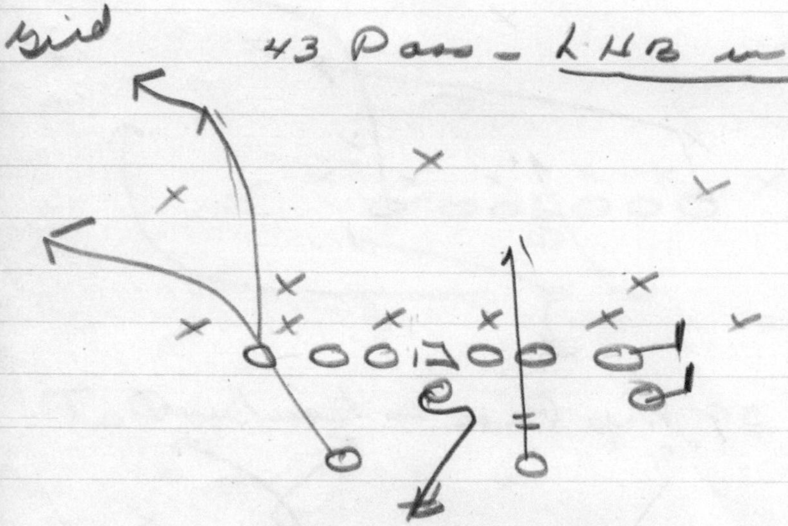

43 Pass - Up

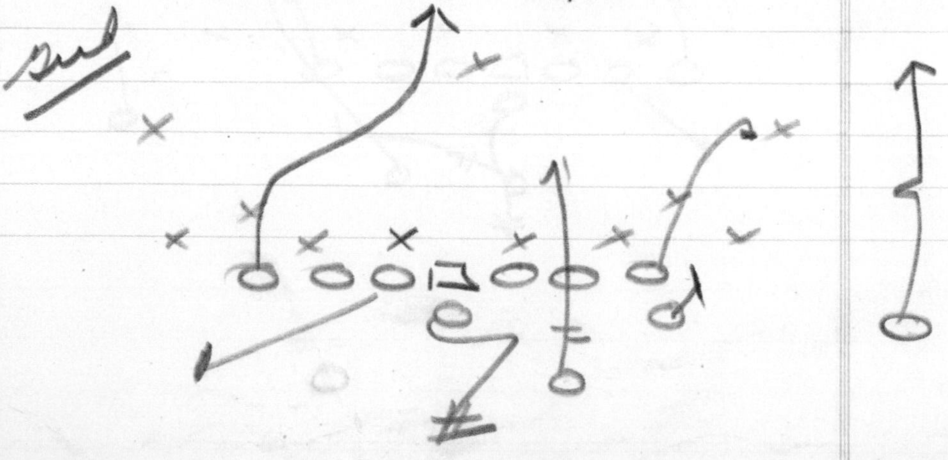

We were running against halfbacks out there. They'd be looking at me coming straight at 'em, and Boyd would be cutting off my tail underneath."

Such plays looked simple, but demanded textbook precision. The spacing and timing of the routes had to be letter-perfect, as Lombardi reminded his receivers *ad nauseum*. "He'd walk around practice, and if he happened to watch passing drills or walk-throughs, if something was fundamentally not sound, he'd correct it," Dale says.

Nothing was too trivial to become a crusade for Lombardi. Dale remembers the coach constantly telling his receivers to come back to the ball if they turned around and found that the pass hadn't yet left the quarterback's hand. If you sit and wait, Lombardi told them, it's a disaster waiting to happen. The defender will have time to break up the pass or intercept. "So he'd scream and yell big-time," Dale says.

In short yardage, Fullback Slant X Post might have been Lombardi's favorite. Starr would fake a running play to the right, then look for the split end, who would run either a fly route or a post depending on the action of the safety to that side.

"If the safety man comes up to play the run, or if he comes up to cover the halfback who is flying down the sideline, the split end runs that post almost directly behind the position that the safety man has vacated. If the safety man drops back, in other words, if he smells pass, the X end will now run a fly downfield," the coach said in *Lombardi on Football*. The Packers ran this play so often during the Lombardi era that many referred to it as the Bart Starr Special. And to his credit, the quarterback usually managed to call it at just the right time. Like in the Ice Bowl.

But never was Lombardi's passing game more radiant than in a 2-minute drill. Here, with the clock winding down and substitutions impossible, is where a well-schooled team truly separated itself from a lesser opponent. "I have spoken throughout of the mental discipline and mental toughness required to win," Lombardi told Flynn. "Nowhere is that more apparent than in those last minutes before the end of the ball

game, or before the end of the half. Great quarterbacks and great teams are at their best here. Watching a team fighting the clock and the opponent as it drives downfield for the winning score is one of the most dramatic moments in a football game and in all of sport. It also tears the guts out of a coach."

Lombardi's Packers spent a great deal of time working on the 2-minute drill. He'd put the ball on the 35-yard line in practice and give the offense 1:30 or 2:00 to get to the far end zone—often against the first-team defense, which, don't forget, knew the plays nearly as well as the offense. The old man was proud to note that, more often than not, his offense won out.

"The passing game is practice and it is precision. That's obvious," he said in *Lombardi on Football*. "What isn't obvious is the persistence: the persistence of the practice field, the persistence of the playbook, the persistence of the quarterback and receivers who must read those defenses and read them correctly, the persistence of those unsung linemen up front who must put on those pass blocks and make them stick, the persistence of the end and flanker and back who must run a route precisely to move their defender to clear an area for the receiver, and the persistence of that receiver to get clear and catch that ball."

Thanks to *his* persistence, as tiresome as it could be at times, the Packers' passing game was effective when it had to be.

OPPOSITE Same basic formation, with three different pass patterns in the 43 Pass series; the right end might block or run a route depending on the variation.
ABOVE Lombardi credited an efficient passing game to practice, precision, and persistence.

5
GREEN MONSTER
LOMBARDI'S DEFENSE

"I'm still a great believer in that old comment that offense sells tickets, and defense wins football games," says Willie Davis, one of Vince Lombardi's team captains. "You go back and follow us very closely, game after game, and probably the last three or four years we were driven by defense."

The thing is, Lombardi, who focused overwhelmingly on offensive strategy and became known as its foremost practitioner, agreed with Davis. "Our primary need was for defensive help," he once said, "because there is nothing more demoralizing to a whole squad than to see the opposition running roughshod over you."

Lombardi was considered a mastermind of offensive game plans when he came to Green Bay, and his nine years with the Packers broadcast that reputation to the world. The power sweep. The play-action pass. Bart Starr channeling the great coach in a tightly choreographed two-minute drill. The dominant images of the era come from the offense. But here are the scores of the Packers' postseason games under Lombardi: 17–13, 37–0, 16–7, 13–10, 23–12, 34–27, 35–10, 28–7, 21–17, 33–14.

With one notable exception, they didn't exactly generate pinball numbers—especially by Green Bay's opponents. Only once did Lombardi's Packers surrender more than 17 points

in a playoff game. Here's another stat, even more amazing: In those ten postseason contests, Green Bay gave up a *total* of only three rushing touchdowns.

Lombardi was full of advice for his defenders. The basics can be found in a document headed SPECIAL DEFENSIVE NOTES (see next spread), which seems to be a holdover from his early days in football, since he illustrates a 4-4-3 defense as "typical" and refers to one linebacker as the fullback, an obsolete term by the 1960s. "You seldom score by defense alone but it is usually good defense that enables you to start your offense in a favorable position," he begins. "Defense is fully as important a factor in winning games as the offense is."

Though the document offers specific guidelines for each player against various offensive sets, it's the more general admonitions that best encapsulate Lombardi's thoughts on the matter. Statements like, "EVERYONE MUST REMEMBER: You do not know in advance what the opposition is going

OPPOSITE Defensive end Willie Davis (87) and defensive tackle Jim Weatherwax (73) bring down Baltimore's Tom Matte. **ABOVE** Lombardi with assistants Bill Austin and Phil Bengtson (right), the architect of the Packers' dominant defense.

SPECIAL DEFENSIVE NOTES

You seldom score by defense alone but it is usually good defense that enables you to start your offense in a favorable position.

Defense is fully as important as a factor in winning games as the offense is. We will just use the following setup as typical:

What is said about this applies to every setup you will use.

1. The linemen must be very definitely set in a very definite position when the ball is passed.
2. The secondary must be alert and instead of being set in a fixed position your position should vary some according to the position on the field, the other tactical factors, and so that the opponents do not know exactly where to find you.

EVERYONE MUST REMEMBER
   1. You do not know in advance what the opposition is going to do.
      (a) They may do anything that can be done in football.
   2. You must be prepared to defend against every conceivable type of play.
   3. If someone definitely tips off the play take advantage of this tip but never try to outguess the QB. HE KNOWS WHAT HE IS CALLING.
   4. Know what you must defend against 1 yd - 3 yds - 5 yds or even 20 yds - BUT AGAIN DO NOT TRY TO GUESS THE PLAY.

All Linemen (except if you are assigned to hang back on pass defense) always take your aggressive initial charge, then close in on the ball carrier and get him.
   You know where that ball is
      1. By seeing it
      2. By the direction in which opposition is attempting to block you. They naturally want to block you away from the ball. So always work into the blocking - never away from it.
      (In case of a conflict between 1 and 2, follow 2)

Be aggressive at the start. Continue that aggressiveness to the extreme so long as ball is coming your way, but if you do not know where ball is or is moving to or if it is going away from you ADD EXTREME CAUTION BUT WITHOUT LOSING AGGRESSIVENESS.

The secondary diagnoses by
      1. Sight of ball
      2. Seeing the blocking in front of them

Barring a punt let's check on the different things the FB may do.
   1. He may have to stop a quick pass in his territory.
   2. " " " " cover an inside back going out on his side.
   3. " " " " drop back and pick up a receiver who is crossing over.
   4. " " " " fade and merely play the ball.
   5. " " " " come up fast.
      (a) Outside the end
      (b) Off tackle
      (c) Inside tackle
      (d) Between guards
      (e) Inside short side tackle

6. He may have to move over more conservatively and prevent a cutback on plays

      (a) off weak side tackle
      (b) around weak side end

His problem is to do the correct one of the above without hesitation and with certainty. DOING THE WRONG THING IS FATAL AND DOING THE RIGHT THING TOO LATE IS ALSO FATAL.

The FB from his position can see the opponents WB, E, FB and TB definitely and maybe the RT and QB (if he lines up in too close a jammed in position he cannot see this - if he lays back too lose he cannot move up in time to properly back the line - HE MUST USE JUDGMENT.

He also can see the ball most of time.

What are some of the real keys for him to act on
1. Ball coming to TB who is fading - this means pass or a delayed run. (Our FB should not rush in - he can take care of his pass covering assignments - and if the play develops into a run can still get up fast enough.
2. Direct pass with ball moving to his flank - this is so easy it needs no comment.
3. Cases where ball is hidden or faked - End and WB are the really important keys.
    (a) Both go thru
        This may be a pass or inside play
    (b) Block your tackle in - play is coming outside of there.

The C from his position can see the opponents T, G. C. QB, TB and FB - and with this should have no trouble diagnosing plays.

The HB's and safety are in a position where they can see everything.

Seeing the ball is valuable - but even if you do not know where the ball is you should be able to tell what the play is quickly.

LE - should see their end work in on our tackle (play outside of there or pass) He cannot tell whether it is outside or inside of him until he sees which way they are trying to block him. He should play into it aggressively.
FB - should see their end work in on our tackle (play outside of there or pass) He should start moving up into the 7 hold and if end is being blocked in widen out.
LT - Charges - pressure comes from his outside and he should work into it. RH is coming in there. Tackle him or stop him with a defensive charge. AND BY NOW YOU SHOULD KNOW WHERE THE BALL IS. GET TO IT.
G - Practically the same problem as LT
RT - Charging on outside shoulder of opposing tackle (who slides thru inside of him) He should see guard pulling away and backs moving to right. BUST IN SHALLOW GETTING TO QB QUICK. (If center contacts him slide across behind own line of scrimmage).

to do. They may do anything that can be done in football." And reminders such as, "If someone definitely tips off the play take advantage of this tip but never try to outguess the QB. HE KNOWS WHAT HE IS CALLING."

The twin engines driving Lombardi's concept of defense were pursuit and tackling. He harped on them constantly. "The heart of a defense is pursuit," he said in *Lombardi on Football.* "Pursuit is dedication. Pursuit is persistence. Pursuit is getting to the ball carrier by taking the shortest course, and when you get there you get there in an angry mood. It is every man's responsibility to pursue until the whistle blows, and when that pursuit has been good and the play ends you can count your team colors around that ball carrier."

And from the same source, here is Lombardi on aggressive tackling: "Defensive football is a game of abandon, and you have to have the kind of players who will be able to play with abandon, the hell-for-leather types. . . . If a man

is running down the street with everything you own, you won't let him get away. That's tackling!"

For all of Lombardi's pontification on defense, and his obvious respect for its importance, he could be surprisingly clueless when it came to his own defensive unit. When the Green Bay offense and defense worked separately—which was during position drills at practice and virtually always in film study—Lombardi invariably gravitated to the offensive side. He would add his two cents to the defense, but the players on that side of the ball secretly smirked that he knew little about their craft.

"During the defensive drills, [defensive coordinator] Phil Bengtson was always right next to him," former linebacker Dave Robinson explains. "What he would do a lot of times, when he saw a play break, he'd say, 'Phil, whose responsibility was that?' Phil would say, 'That was Robinson.' And he'd say, 'Robinson, what the hell are you doing?!'"

ABOVE Linebacker Ray Nitschke (second from left) and defensive teammates at San Francisco's Kezar Stadium in 1960.

Robinson remembers Lombardi getting into stance one time and demonstrating to him how to use his right forearm instead of his left forearm on a certain play. Robinson is convinced Bengtson showed it to Lombardi beforehand.

At first glance, there is contradiction between Lombardi's seeming neglect of his defense and the great things it did on the field. The main reason it all worked was Bengtson. While it's true the hyper-organized Lombardi had command of every phase of the operation, he did know how to delegate.

Bengtson was part of Lombardi's original Green Bay staff, and he was an unsung hero of Titletown. He ran defensive meetings, named starters, and made defensive calls during games—signaling them in to middle linebacker Ray Nitschke, usually with just a finger or two or three. In many ways, Bengtson was the antidote to Lombardi's bluster. He was tall, lean, and unflappable, more of a professor than a preacher. "It was an unbelievable contrast," says Jim Temp, who played defensive end under Bengtson for two seasons. "Phil was so laidback, I don't think I ever heard him say [shoot]."

When Lombardi stepped down as head coach after the 1967 season and Bengtson filled his shoes, those low-key personality traits weren't necessarily an advantage. The handpicked successor was a mediocre 20-21-1 in three seasons in charge of the Packers, a record that tarnished his reputation somewhat.

But his former underlings remain fairly unanimous in their praise of Lombardi's right-hand man. "Phil Bengtson was the finest defensive man I've ever known in roughly 25 years in the NFL," says Jerry Burns, Green Bay's defensive backs coach in 1966-67. "I know Lombardi trusted him without question."

Not that Lombardi was completely divorced from the defensive side. "I never personally thought Vince had a great defensive mind," Robinson says. "He had a great offensive mind. But what he could do, when he saw a weakness in the defense, he knew to take advantage of it. When you saw a play work, he'd say, 'How can we stop that play?'"

In 1967, Robinson recalls, the Giants took advantage of one of his tendencies to pull him inside and get their halfback free outside. Lombardi was convinced Green Bay's next opponent, St. Louis, would see the defect and try to exploit it, so he had his defense practice against the play repeatedly. Sure enough, the Cardinals ran the play, and the Packers stopped it. Next week, same thing. What really impressed Robinson is that four or five weeks later—he can't remember the opponent—when the play was all but forgotten, Lombardi came to him and said, "Dave, remember that play New York ran against us? Well, I look for these guys to run that play against you."

"Sure enough, first play of the game, there it was," Robinson says. "And he'd do stuff like that to make you say, 'This man is awesome.'"

However you might apportion the praise, the Packers' defense in the Lombardi era was a model of simplicity. The defensive linemen didn't stunt much (in other words, they tended to work against the blocker directly in front of them instead of attempting to loop behind a teammate to a different gap), and the defensive backs didn't mix a whole lot of different coverages. Lombardi hated the prevent defense, and would usually keep only four defensive backs on the field for opponents' two-minute drills.

"It was very, very simple," Temp says. "You had your position. And when the ball was snapped, you had your keys."

"Our concept was, and Vince drove this home to us, don't give up more than three yards on any one play," Robinson says. "It's first-and-10, then it's second-and-7, then third-and-4, then fourth-and-1 and they have to punt."

The old linebacker has a hard time watching the bend-but-don't-break defenses of the new century, most of which play cautious Cover 2 schemes and bank on the idea that offenses won't be able to string together twenty plays on a scoring drive. They don't mind occasionally giving up 10 or 15 yards. "Some of these teams today, Vince would have had a coronary," Robinson says.

The Packers were a highly effective blitzing team when they chose to be. In Super Bowl I, for example, they waited until the second half to call their first blitz against Kansas

City, and they tipped Len Dawson's pass on the play; safety Willie Wood picked off the wobbling ball and took it to the Chiefs' 5-yard line. But the Packers simply didn't blitz much. Robinson says that in 1966, the first Super Bowl season, they averaged three blitzes per game. And when they did, it was always a linebacker, never a defensive back.

And yet if the system was vanilla in some ways, there was flexibility built into it. When Robinson was traded to Washington in 1973, Redskins coach George Allen called him into his office and showed him some Packers film. "What defense is this?" Allen asked on one play. Robinson told him.

"What about on the other side?" Allen asked. "Same one," Robinson replied. "But they're not doing the same thing," the incredulous Allen told him.

Robinson explained that in Green Bay, the players adapted their defensive packages to the strengths and weaknesses of individual players. For example, Davis hated getting hit low by the tight end; it threw him off his game. So when the tight end lined up right, Robinson would make sure he never got to Davis. On the other side, defensive end Lionel Aldridge actually liked working off a pressing tight end. So when the tight end lined up left, the outside linebacker to that side, Lee Roy Caffey, would let him go.

It was the same defensive call, but the play looked completely different depending on the offensive alignment. It took intuition on the part of the Packers' defenders, and that came from years of playing together and good communication.

Underlying all of it was an exceptional collection of talent. A dozen different Green Bay defenders made the Pro Bowl during the Lombardi era, and six of them—Davis, Nitschke, Wood, defensive tackle Henry Jordan, safety Emlen Tunnell, and cornerback Herb Adderley—are in the Pro Football Hall of Fame.

The stars of the defensive line clearly were Jordan and Davis, both obtained in trades with Cleveland. Lombardi liked his defensive tackles to line up 18 inches off the ball, unless it was a short-yardage play. In that case they would close the gap. He prized quickness over mass

at this position, and no one was quicker off the ball than Jordan. Davis, one of Green Bay's first African-American stars, was one of the NFL's most relentless pass rushers. The 1961 NFL Championship Game was a good indication. The Giants tried to block Davis with three different offensive tackles—first rookie Greg Larson, then Mickey Walker and finally Jack Stroud, who was moved from a guard position. None of them could keep him out of the backfield.

Behind the line, the Packers' linebackers had manifold responsibilities. "We expect the linebacker to be strong enough to fight off the blocks of those big offensive linemen and quick enough to get to that ball carrier," the coach said in *Lombardi on Football*. "He must also learn patience and be patient enough to wait and read, and alert enough to understand his keys, recognize the run and close the hole. He must also be fast enough, once he reads pass, to be able to cover the tight ends and the backs coming out of the backfield."

"And he didn't tell it all," Robinson says.

Lombardi graded all his players on a scale from +2 to -2. If you carried out your assignment as scripted and didn't do anything spectacular, you got a 0. Intercept a pass and you were likely to receive a +2; a blown coverage might net you -2. "He told me a good score for a linebacker is minus-four in a ball game," Robinson says. "That's because you had so many responsibilities on you. He told me this during [contract] negotiations. We had fourteen games, so that meant minus-56 for the year was an average year."

The next year, in 1966, Robinson was back for negotiations, and Lombardi made the mistake of pulling the linebacker's file and noting that his score for the season was +26. "I said, 'I'm getting my raise this year,'" Robinson recalls. "It didn't work out that way, but I got a lot more than he originally intended to give me."

Green Bay had a number of solid outside linebackers during Lombardi's tenure—especially the athletic Robinson, who showed up in 1963. But the constant was the menacing presence in the middle: Nitschke. If men like Davis were the

brains of the Packers' defense and swift defensive backs like Adderley were the legs, Nitschke was its pulsing heart.

"The thing that would help us corners is the guys running the across patterns, they had to look for him," defensive back Jesse Whittenton says. "And he didn't let up too often."

In the secondary, things were typically uncluttered. "We had a 4-3 key, which was man-to-man," Whittenton says, running through the coverage options. "We had the red dog [or blitz]; that was man, but you didn't expect help. And we had zone—but Lombardi didn't like zone too much."

Whittenton and his pals had to be versatile, though. Lombardi laid out his ambitions for his defensive backs in a short treatise labeled PASS DEFENSE. Among his points (also seen on the following pages): "Must be aggressive—a thrown ball is a free ball," "Under no circumstances let a man get behind you," and "Know down, distance, time."

Underscoring each with a red wavy line and embellishing his message with details, Lombardi then goes on

to spell out two pages of instructions just on the play of the safeties.

But the Green Bay DBs weren't simply pass defenders. In that rugged era, everyone was expected to tackle soundly. In *Lombardi on Football*, the coach says of Wood, "pound for pound, he was our hardest tackler."

As is often the case with great teams, though, the individual attributes of the Packers' defenders didn't fully explain their success. Under Bengtson's tutelage and Lombardi's hectoring, the Green Bay defense had a synergy that has rarely been duplicated over the years. "When the going got kind of tough, we'd get into the huddle and say, 'Guys, if we're gonna win this, we gotta do something.' And we'd pick it up," Davis says. "Next thing you know, we get an interception or a big tackle or a fumble or something. But we clearly had a sense that when it was necessary, we could be very instrumental in winning. And I'll tell you right now, that came from Coach Lombardi also."

ABOVE Safety Willie Wood (24) helps Willie Davis (87) stand up the Lions' Mel Farr in a game at Detroit in 1968.

①

PASS DEFENSE

① Must be aggressive - a thrown
ball is a free ball

② Under no circumstances let a
man get behind you
   a) Stick with man in your
zone until he cuts out, there let
him go - at same time look
for a receiver crossing into
your zone

③ turn toward your own goal
line with receiver - however
always keep eyes on passer; never
let him out of your sight. Stay
with receiver until ball is in
air.

④ Never let receiver get closer than
3 yds - (leaves you vulnerable
to fake)

⑤ Half Back stay deep on passes.
in flat until ball is in air
∴ by toward ball when
thrown regardless of how far
away it seems. to be - as a
Tackler on a blocker

The First thought of a
defensive secondary is "It is going
to be a pass until positive
it is a run. Half Back usually
will be up fast enough on
running plays anyway. You
can never catch a receiver who
gets behind you

⑥ Know down, distance, time. Ends
will help you diagnose plays.
a little faster; if End blocks;
if he flies out expect pass.

⑦ Half Back should try to keep
everything to inside - if
caught Safety man is there

③

⑧ Safety men must be conservative. More in fact once certain. If Half Backs is behind Receiver it is possible for Safety men to move in front for interception.

Safety men must cover the inside men.

⑨ Speak e.g. end across

⑩ Two Receivers in zone, the Half Backs responsibility is the outside one or the deep one.

⑪ Never take eyes of the Passer and the Ball; go toward the ball when thrown

SAFETY MAN

The defensive scheme today is a coordinated one. Eleven men are a unit.

The Safety Mans position has remained constant

① The most important
② Every play envolves gain or loss of long yardage.

Play

① Lineman on error - 10 men will cover
② Line Backers on error - 2 H Bs 1 S M.
③ Half Backs " " - Safety Man
④ Safety Man " " - T. D.

The average is 8 punts per game - 5 will be returned.

Passes

- Passes 18 - 20 yds deep.
- Center Zone at 15 yds.
- Deep behind Half Backs.
- favor the strong side

6

BLOCK THAT KICK

LOMBARDI'S SPECIAL TEAMS

Before there was such a thing as a special-teams coach—
Dick Vermeil is generally credited as the first, with the Los Angeles Rams in 1969—Vince Lombardi was a coach who appreciated special teams.

"One of the most important parts of football is the kicking game," he told editor George Flynn for the *Lombardi on Football* set. "It is also one that gets the least attention in the press and in the reporting by the experts who cover the games on radio and television. But without a sound kicking game and also the excellent specialty teams that make the kicking game successful, the chances of winning a championship are slight."

It made sense that special teams—placekicking, punting, kickoffs, kick coverage, and returns—would appeal to Lombardi. As he alluded, the parts of the game that fell outside the headings of Offense and Defense tended to be overlooked. Lombardi appreciated the humble worker drones of the game, and he saw that kick returns and coverage required precise coordination, another of his hallmarks. He also knew that the thirty to forty plays carried out by his special teams in each game were critical to the team's fortunes. "In the closest football games, some part of the kicking game will be the deciding factor," he once said, as quoted by his son in *The Essential Vince Lombardi*.

Just a couple examples came against the Vikings in 1963, and against the Rams in the 1967 Western Conference Championship Game. In the former, Adderley charged in from Minnesota's left with about 2:00 left and blocked a field-goal attempt; Green Bay's Hank Gremminger picked it up and ran for a clinching touchdown. In the playoff game, Los Angeles was trying to push its lead to 10–0 when Dave Robinson and Henry Jordan got a big push up the middle and Robinson swatted a field-goal try. The Packers went on to win 28–7.

Like most coaches of the day, Lombardi had no qualms about putting some of his best players on the field to block on a kickoff return or chase down a punt. Willie Wood was his primary punt returner for most of Lombardi's tenure in Green Bay, and Herb Adderley shared kickoff returns for seven years. Both doubled as Hall of Fame defensive backs. Before specialist Don Chandler showed up in 1965, star halfback Paul Hornung and starting guard Jerry Kramer did the

OPPOSITE Holder Bart Starr watches the flight of the ball on a kick by Paul Hornung. **ABOVE** Hornung kicks off against the Giants in a 1961 game at Milwaukee. Number 33 is Lew Carpenter.

69

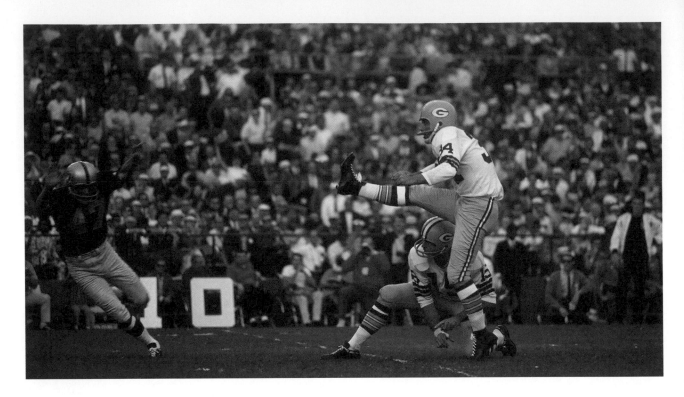

placekicking. Receivers Max McGee and Boyd Dowler each spent time as the team's punter.

Lombardi kept an outline of instructions for his kicking game on two legal-sized sheets of yellow paper (see next spread). "(1) Punt—important—10 to 15 times per game," he wrote. Points (a) and (b) beneath Punt are "Center pass—spiral, target—1 sec to 1.2 secs," and "Punter mechanics—born not made."

Not that Lombardi trusted the matter to genetics. He did his best to mold good special-teams players with detailed orders. Here are his instructions for long snaps, from *Lombardi on Football*: "The center grips the ball on the laces with his right hand as a passer would. His left hand is at the back of the ball and is his guiding hand. As he becomes more experienced he'll be able to move that left hand forward to add more power and speed but until then he must sacrifice some of that speed for accuracy. As the ball is centered it is spun so that it reaches the kicker on a spiral, arriving at that belt-high level on line with the kicking leg."

His directions to the punter were even more exacting, with guidelines on positioning the ball, striding, dropping the ball to the foot, contact and follow-through. "If the punt is properly executed, a good long spiraling kick can be heard as well as seen," he said. "It will sound more like a thud than a big boom."

Lombardi was ahead of his time when it came to punting strategy. Through his reign, punters almost always simply drove the ball as far as they could, which explains the high punting averages of the 1940s, 1950s and 1960s. Lombardi was willing to sacrifice distance for height, knowing that a high punt gave the return man less chance of breaking a long one.

In 1967, his final season in Green Bay, the Packers allowed just 22 return yards on 13 punts—a ridiculously low average of 1.7 yards per return. The longest punt return against them that season was 10 yards. Lombardi knew these stats well, and was quite proud of them.

He was a trendsetter in one other regard. In *Lombardi on Football*, he said: "To my way of thinking, the kickers have

ABOVE Don Chandler nails a field goal against the Raiders in Super Bowl II at Miami's Orange Bowl.

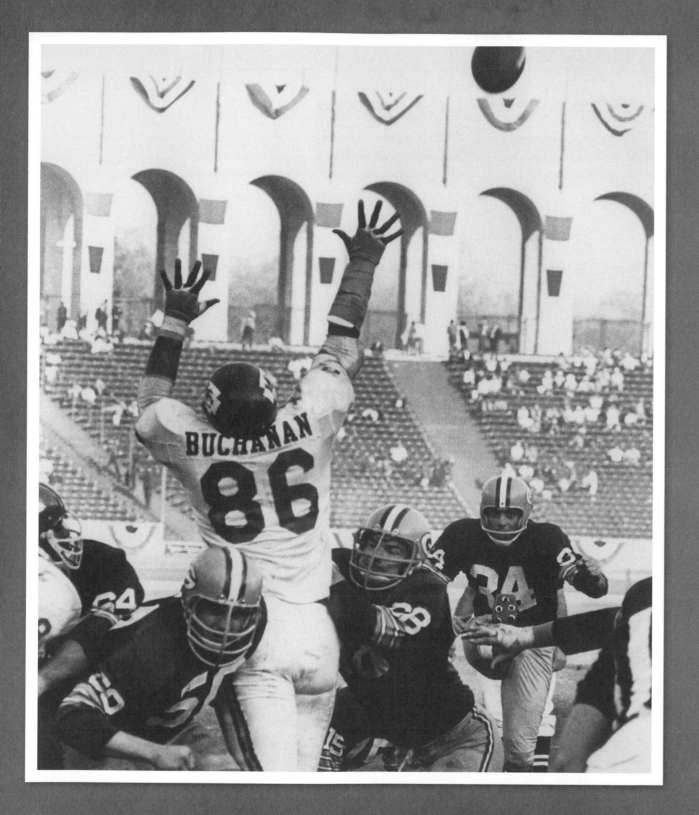

ABOVE Chandler's extra-point attempt easily clears the massive wingspan of Kansas City's Buck Buchanan in Super Bowl I.

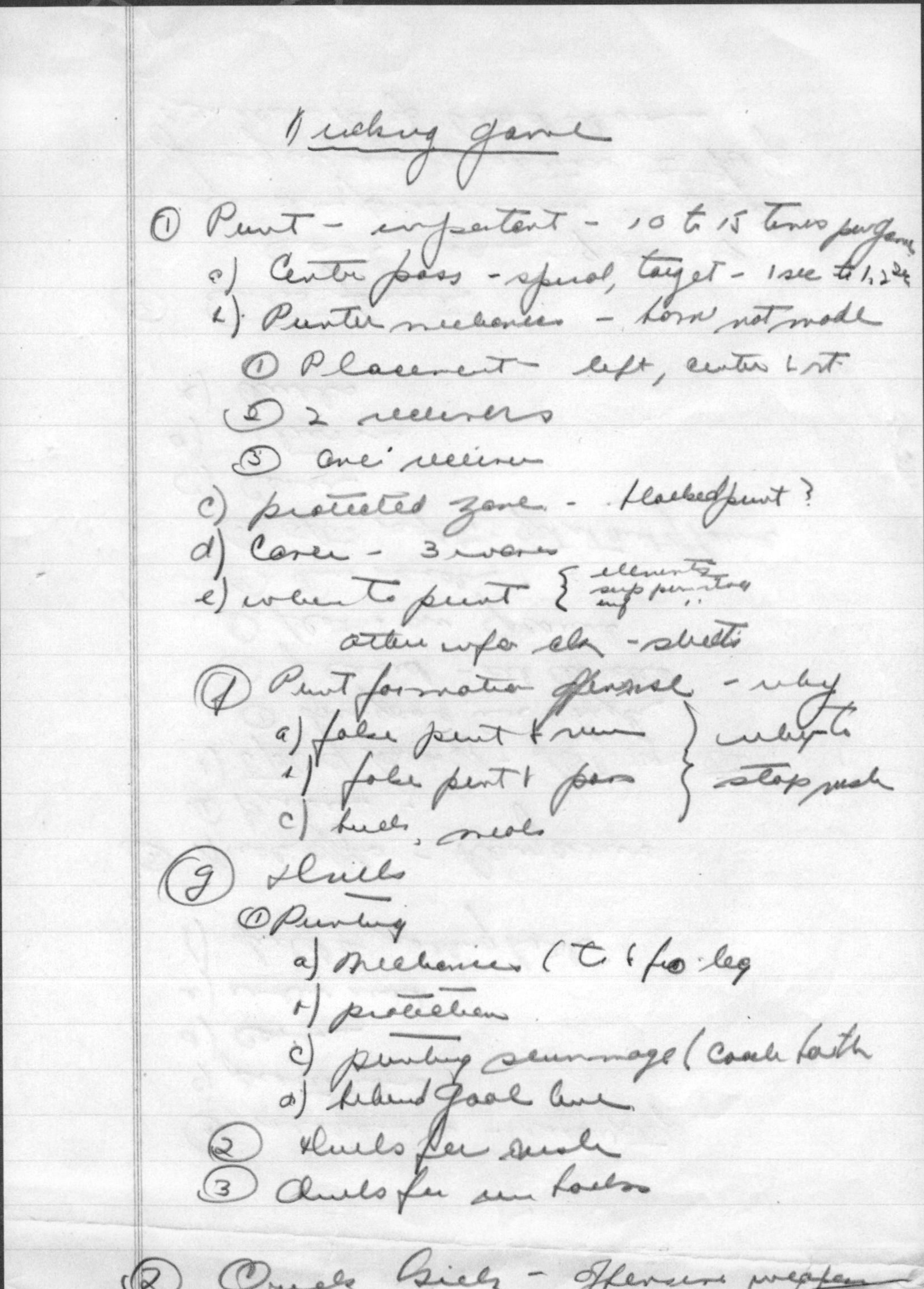

Kicking game

① Punt - important - 10 to 15 times per game
   a) Center pass - spiral, target - 1 sec to 1,2 yd
   b) Punter mechanics - born, not made
      ① Placement - left, center & rt
      ② 2 receivers
      ③ one receiver
   c) protected zone - Blocked punt ?
   d) Cover - 3 waves
   e) when to punt { elements sup pun tog
         attn wfr cln - stretti

⑥ Punt formation spread - why
   a) false punt & run } unbefto
   b) false punt & pass } stop rush
   c) heels, meals

Ⓖ Skills
   ① Punting
     a) Mechanics (& for leg
     b) protection
     c) punting scrimmage (coach both
     d) defend goal line
   ② Skills for snaps
   ③ Skills for sure toebox

② Onside kick - offensive weapon

b) mechanics - Crossoverstep.
c) protection
d) Cover
e) when used
f) field a rolling ball

③ Kick offs. - Rangers
a) kicker -
1) type of kick off - flat reg. tee
① on goal line : high
② placed - all direction
③ flat : on ground
④ On side -
⑤ after safety - get it out of bounds
c) Cover
d) returns
e) drills

④ Extra points
cool man - good leg.
under pressure - show
fingers in practice to help
center keep head down

improved to such an extent that too many kickoffs are going so deep into the end zone that the runback is going the way of the quick kick. . . . As a fan, if the kickoff team were moved back to the 35-yard line to insure more runbacks, I'd applaud."

The league took his advice and moved the kickoff line from the 40 in 1974.

On kickoffs, Lombardi wanted his return team to build a five-man wedge in the middle of the field and push the rest of the interference to the periphery. He would have his two guards, stationed on the frontline at about the 40, crisscross so that they may be angled to drive their men outside.

The coach liked to have two deep men for kickoffs. And even though these tended to be lean, swift players, and sometimes valuable, whichever one didn't field the ball was expected to race forward and join the wedge. Lombardi wanted any kickoff that went deeper than five yards in the end zone to be downed for a touchback.

As for punt returns, each one would be set up to go either right or left. "Up the middle is the shortest way to the other goal line, but on a punt return, unlike the kickoff

ABOVE Starr and Chandler practice their holds and footing on the "frozen tundra" before a game at Lambeau Field.

PUNT RETURNS

The idea of a dedicated special teams coach was still foreign when Lombardi prowled the sidelines, but he took great interest and pride in the Packers' kicking game. He had coaching points on all the major aspects of special teams—punting, kickoffs, placekicks, and kick coverage.

Here are a couple different punt-return plays drawn in the coach's hand, and they employ subtly different formations. The front line is set up the same in both, and each calls for two deep men. But the top formation has one player at linebacker depth and two upbacks; those numbers are reversed in the bottom formation.

In the first example, most of the defensive linemen rush, then take a looping path back into the Packers' side of the play. There they set up a return to the right. The return men aren't assigned arrows, but you can presume one of them will try to get around the right edge while his blockers form a wall and force the action toward the middle of the field.

The second example looks more serious about blocking the punt, with the two interior linemen taking outside rushes and the linebackers overwhelming the center in the middle. The blocking for the return is very symmetrical, meaning it could probably go to the left or right with equal efficiency.

Punt return

Tackles and Ends out

Rules off Return

x

4   3   2   1 x 1 2 3 4 5

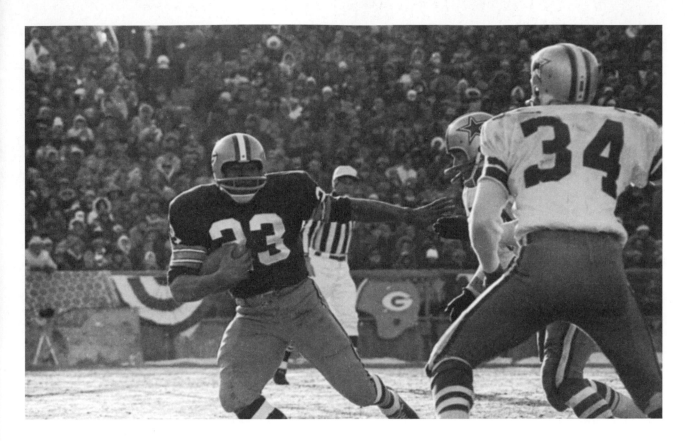

return, the defensive line is right on top of your running back and you can seldom get to the center of the field," he told Flynn. "Also, on the kickoff return, you've got time to form a wedge and take advantage of the better blocking." Lombardi asked his punt returners to loop backward a few yards, giving the blockers a chance to form their screen. Up at the line, he usually wanted only two outside men to rush the opponent's punter.

The Packers' special teams were always solid under Lombardi. But they gained a flash of brilliance in 1967, his last year, when he drafted Travis Williams out of Arizona State. Williams was a troubled soul who would battle substance abuse and die at the age of forty-five. But he was the Devin Hester of his day, a sensation in the open field.

Williams averaged 41.1 yards per kickoff returns as a rookie, with four touchdowns. Both still stand as all-time records, though the touchdown mark was tied once. He returned consecutive kickoffs for scores in the first quarter of a game against Cleveland, helping Green Bay to a 35–7 lead. "Williams had that great breakaway speed that is so necessary to be able to run kickoffs the length of the field," the coach said in *Lombardi on Football*. "He had the strength in the legs and in the shoulders to be able to get past the tacklers, and was able to spot the daylight and run to it."

And the Packers had their tricks, too. McGee shocked Philadelphia in the 1960 NFL Championship Game by faking a punt and running around left end for 35 yards on fourth-and-10. The play set up Bart Starr's touchdown pass to McGee, though the Eagles came back to win.

Lombardi gave his punter the OK to run when he saw an opportunity. Just as with his offense, the Green Bay special teams played conservatively and predictably until you let your guard down. Then they would strike.

OPPOSITE A designed kickoff return up the middle; note how the front linemen cross to the opposite sides of the field for better blocking angles.
ABOVE Brilliant kickoff returner Travis Williams (23) displays his flair for footwork in a short yardage gain against the Cowboys in the 1967 title game.

77

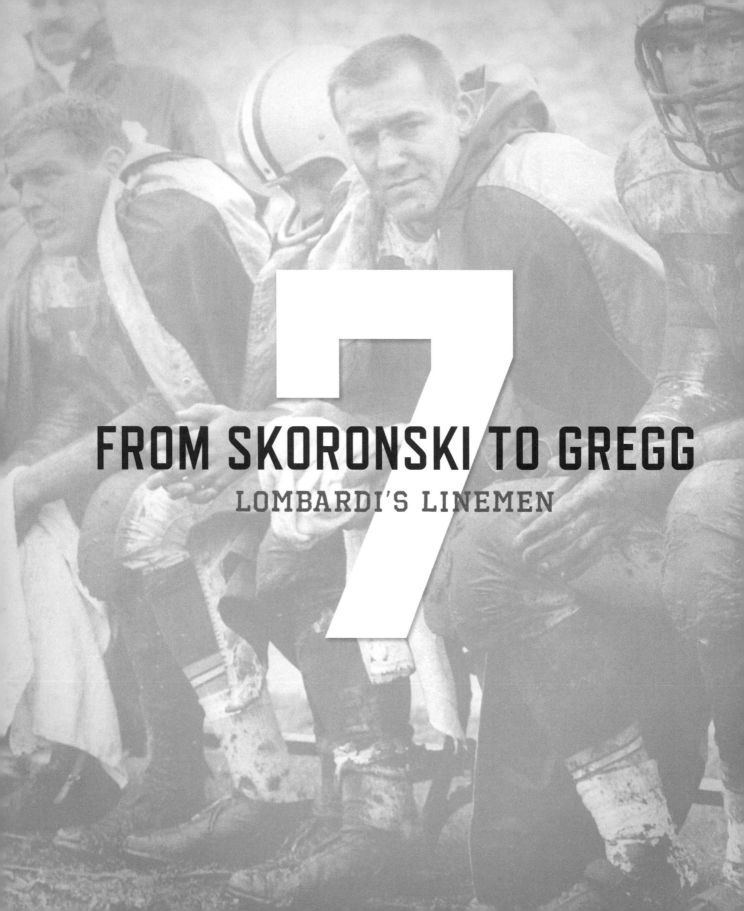

7
FROM SKORONSKI TO GREGG
LOMBARDI'S LINEMEN

Vince Lombardi played right guard in his college days at Fordham, and he always identified with offensive linemen. This was the blessing of the Green Bay Packers' blockers, and no doubt their lasting curse.

Most of the Packers hoped for nothing more than to escape the attention of the occasionally volcanic Lombardi, both on the practice field and during games. The offensive linemen had little chance. "He didn't work so much with us individually," says former lineman Forrest Gregg. "He'd move around to all parts of the game. After offense, he'd move over to defense—which we were all happy about. But he did spend a lot of time with us."

Gregg was the portable emergency kit of the Packers' O-line. His primary position was right tackle, but he also played left tackle or guard when the team needed him to—and excelled at all of them. And he acknowledges that Lombardi probably focused more closely on his guards than any other position.

Jerry Kramer, Green Bay's right guard, is sure of it. "Fuzzy (Thurston) and I sat down and talked about it," Kramer says. "Because he was an offensive lineman and not a back; because he was a guard, and not a tackle or a center; because he was a *right* guard, I felt there wasn't any question—he might not know how to play safety or quarterback or something he'd

never played. But he felt damn sure he knew how to play right guard, and I felt he gave it a little special attention."

The truth of it was that Lombardi was somewhat partial to all his offensive linemen, and he assembled quite a group in Green Bay. It's remarkable how long most of them stayed together. The same five stalwarts formed the Green Bay front wall from 1960–63, four of Lombardi's nine seasons. They were Bob Skoronski at left tackle, Thurston at left guard, Jim Ringo at center, Kramer at right guard, and Gregg at right tackle. They were, in fact, the heart of the offensive line during Lombardi's tenure, though only Gregg started all nine seasons. Even their replacements, like center Ken Bowman or tackle Norm Masters, tended to be long-time Packers.

Each had a distinct personality and an appointed role in the Packers' locker room. Skoronski was the heart of the line, a big lug known to tear up when the emotion hit him. Kramer was sort of the poet-philosopher of Titletown, a man

OPPOSITE Offensive lineman Forrest Gregg (75) sits next to fullback Jim Taylor on the bench in a game at San Francisco. **ABOVE** Lombardi could dole out praise at Tuesday film sessions, but he gave linemen hell for missing a block.

79

who went on to become a successful author. Gregg was the fierce loyalist, and technically the soundest player of the bunch. Thurston was champion drinker and lovable class clown. "He has a talent for rhyming, and when he bellows out a calypso account of his personal heroics, he doesn't need a mike," Lombardi once wrote of Fuzzy.

Former wide receiver Boyd Dowler roomed with Thurston on the road. In Super Bowl I, the left guard was saddled with the responsibility of blocking Chiefs defensive tackle Buck Buchanan, who blotted out the sun at 6'7", 270 pounds. Thurston was listed at 6'1", 247. Dowler, meanwhile, got hurt very early in the game, and wound up watching from the sidelines.

At one point, he noticed Thurston standing near him, his facemask bent at a peculiar angle. "What's up?" Dowler asked him.

"If you were blocking that big SOB, your facemask would be bent, too," Fuzzy roared at him. "You're not doing anything but standing over here."

After a pregnant pause, Dowler asked his roommate, "So how are you doing with him?"

"I'm kicking his ass," Thurston replied slyly.

Lombardi's offensive linemen were more than sitcom characters, of course, or they wouldn't have lasted so long in his system. Gregg and Ringo are in the Pro Football Hall of Fame, Kramer has appeared on the final ballot, and quarterback Bart Starr has said he believed Skoronski should be in the Hall, too. Whether they would have gotten there without Lombardi is another question. "After two years of professional football, I was not an accomplished offensive lineman," Gregg says. "I think I more or less developed under him and his system. I have to give him a lot of credit."

Not that Lombardi spent an inordinate amount of one-on-one time with his blockers. "Very rarely would he talk to you about specific assignments," Kramer says. "It was more when you screwed up, he'd be all over your case. And once in a while, when you threw a great block or something, he'd cheer."

ABOVE Lombardi congratulates left tackle Bob Skoronski after the Packers win Super Bowl I.

More often, Lombardi—always a liberal delegator—worked through his line coaches. From 1959-1964 that was Bill Austin, who had played guard under Lombardi with the Giants. When Austin left, Ray Wietecha, who had played center for Lombardi with the Giants, took over. "Once in a while he would demonstrate something," former guard Gale Gillingham says of Lombardi. "Mostly it came to Ray, and through Ray to us."

The play of any offensive line revolves around communication, and the stability of Lombardi's line helped tremendously in this regard. As with most teams, it began with the center. "Ringo would call it odd or even," former tight end Ron Kramer says. "The two guards and two tackles had to determine who would take who, and I'd have to determine which guy I would take. And we had to do it while these [defensive] guys are shifting around, like two seconds before the snap."

"For example on our sweep, if he called even he was gonna do an outside cutoff, and the tackle was gonna move to the middle linebacker," Gillingham says. "If it was odd, the tackle would come down on the defensive tackle, and Bow went for the linebacker. And then there would be things one of us or the other would see on the outside. There was a lot of conversation up there."

The center had the leeway to change his line call if the defense shifted before the snap, but the Packers didn't do a whole lot of that. They usually felt they could block any scheme with the original call.

Even after the snap, though, the blocking assignments could change. "You may think, whatever the center called, that was it," Gillingham says. "But you may be at right guard and end up picking the [opposite] outside linebacker up depending on which play-action was called. . . . If you didn't think you could handle the way the [opponent] was lined up, then it would go odd, even though you kind of weren't."

Got it? You can see why it took a while to blossom.

All of Lombardi's offensive linemen were important in his system, but the guards became its epitome. They were certainly the most visible, barreling around the edge on the famed power sweep. The Packers ran the ball more than most teams, and Thurston and Jerry Kramer—or at least one of them—pulled or trapped on a majority of Lombardi's plays.

"The guards are the focal point of the offense," the coach told *Sports Illustrated* in 1964. "Everything they do is critical. They open the holes for the quick openers, break the way for the sweeps and bodyguard the passer."

In that same story, one opponent told the magazine of Thurston: "I just can't shake that man. He's like a kid brother—always in the way."

Lombardi was a stickler for proper technique at every position on the field, and his notes include pages of handwritten assignments for play after play (see CENTER ASSIGNMENTS, next page). He was especially demanding of his offensive linemen. "Good offensive line play is based on good stance, explosive start, body control, correct hitting position on contact, a forceful delivery of the blow and the follow-through," he told editor George Flynn. "When the offensive line comes off the ball, it must come off not like the keys of a typewriter but as one man. Uniformity in line play is an absolute necessity. . . . There is only way to execute each block—the correct way."

ABOVE The boss hammers home a point to offensive line coach Bill Austin.

<u>Center</u>.

49-28   —   'O' man, move for Back

69-68   (CP may be necessary to cut off inside)

39-38

39-38 Dip

29-48 P.O. — Release outside man over you,

     move 1st man to outside + seal inside

39-38 Sucker — Drive offside unless 'o' man

43-22   over you with MM, L.B. then drive

63-62   this "O" man (R.P. - 52 defense)

41-20 Trap

61-60 Trap   Draw 5 - Draw 4

47-26   —   'O' man, if over, move drive offside

65-64   (CP - 43 defense - may Block add)

F35 - F34   Middle Screen

57-56 option — 'O' man, move inside S or H.B.

67-66

37-36

77-76

B47 - B26

45-24 Cross — 'O' man, move seal offside

55-54

B35 - B34

Center-

F31-F30 — Drive offside

43-22 ~~~~ C.P. (-)

41-20 quick — 'O' man if over you,
61-60 quick   none drive offside
51-50
B31- B30
51 - 50 Co

Reverse left & Right
St. left & Right odd - check & release inside
                  even - cut off inside

Draw Right & left — Set as on Pass, then Drive
                   man over in direction of angle,
                   none drive offside

Middle Screen -

ABOVE Lombardi believed that practically anything could be accomplished through several hundred hours on the blocking sled.

A more detailed picture of Lombardi's approach emerges through a typed document titled simply, FOOTBALL BLOCKING (next spread). "About 75% of all offensive football is BLOCKING," Lombardi states. He then runs through stance, approach, contact, and follow-through, describing conditions under which blocks are made and breaking down different types of blocks.

If the Green Bay offensive linemen were expected to best their opponents one-on-one, that wasn't the end of it. Remember, if Lombardi's play book was fairly simple, assignments could be complex.

Slightly up the complexity scale were what he called pinch blocks or double-team blocks. These were primarily used to drive defensive linemen backward on short-yardage plays. The "post man" would plant his head into the defender's midsection to break his charge, while the "pinch man" would hit the victim from the side and prevent him from rolling away.

Lombardi also had a technique for his center called the look-and-see block. On plays like the basic off-tackle play, the center was supposed to pause for a fraction of a second and read the movement of the middle linebacker. If the opponent blitzed over him, the snapper was to pick him up; if the middle linebacker took off in pursuit of the back, the center was to block down on the offside defensive tackle.

More important to Lombardi's overall scheme was option blocking, or rule blocking. "Instead of squaring off as they had in the past with the opposite man and locking horns like two giant dinosaurs, the option-blocker was expected to contact his opponent to determine the thrust of the opponent's drive and assist him in that direction," he told Flynn. "In other words, 'take him in the direction he wants to go.'"

Option blocking was the cornerstone of Lombardi's "run to daylight" philosophy. The blocker would quickly gauge a potential tackler's momentum, and simply steer him in that direction. It was up to the ball carrier to read the block and make the appropriate cut. These blocks made the Packers' plays flexible, which made them exceedingly difficult to disrupt.

And then there were do-dad blocks, perhaps the height of Lombardi choreography. Sometimes called area blocks, they were used against stunting defensive lines or defenses that liked to stack one man behind another. Simply stated, do-dads were variable tag-team blocks, by two offensive players against two specific defenders.

For example, the center and left guard might be responsible for the middle linebacker and the onside defensive tackle on a weakside handoff to the fullback. But the two offensive linemen wouldn't know which of them was responsible for which guy until after the snap of the ball. Both would fire out toward the defensive tackle. If he took an inside charge, the center would pick him up and the guard would hunt for the middle linebacker; if he took an outside charge, the roles would be reversed.

On film, if executed properly, do-dad blocking looked reflexive. In reality, the blocking duos had to be on precisely the same page mentally, and that sprang from endless repetition. "We practiced them nonstop," Gillingham says. "It was completely foreign to me. We had done nothing like that in college. Ray [Wietecha] would have us in our groups, and we'd practice that stuff until it was automatic. And of course they filmed everything. You'd review it over and over. You knew that stuff in your sleep."

Do-dad blocking in particular, and the Packers' line play in general, exposed one of the great lies in pro football. Offensive linemen, because of their size, normally proportioned egos and occasionally passive nature, are often seen as the dumb plow horses of the NFL. The truth is much the opposite. Their play requires a higher level of coordination and thought than most other positions.

And with Lombardi, the old guard, driving them, the Green Bay linemen weren't going to be anything less than flawless. "I know this: He expected a lot from us," Gregg says. "And those expectations were the reason we had a good, solid offensive line."

Quite an understatement from the lynchpin of what might have been the greatest line in NFL history.

FOOTBALL BLOCKING

About 75% of all offensive football is BLOCKING. There are two phases to every block regardless of what its nature is.

    1. Preliminaries
    2. Final

1. Involves:
    a. Stance from which you start
    b. Approach to position
    c. Contact
2. Involves:
    a. Continuity and follow up of the block.

1. (a) Stance from which you start.
    It must: 1. Enable you to start fast
           2. Enable you to cover up your intentions
           3. Enable you to move firmly in any direction.
  (b) Approach to position
    You must move fast and accurately always having your body
        balanced and under control
  (c) Contact
    Must be solid, must be accurate, must be made with snap, and
        must be made with your body balanced and under control

2. (a) Continuity and follow up of the block (without this, the prelim-
    inaries are wasted). The block must always be continued with
    as much power as possible UNTIL THE REASON FOR MAKING THE
    BLOCK HAS VANISHED.

There are three general conditions under which blocks are made.

    1. Close blocking (man on line of scrimmage blocking an op-
        ponent on line of scrimmage)
    2. Semi-open blocking (where blocker must move several steps
        to make his block; but where the spot of the block is
        fairly well defined.
    3. Open blocking (where blocker must move at least several
        steps to the location of his block and where the spot of
        making his block is not well defined in advance.

The more common types of close blocking are

    1. Shoulder block.
      a. Generally used when you want to drive a defensive man
        out of position. Regardless of what the defensive man
        is going to do, getting to him fast pays dividends.
        (a) It helps your power to be moving fast
        (b) The quicker you get to him the more stationary your
          target is; and consequently, the more accurate
          you will be.

b. Points to be remembered.
   1. Drive off with an initial lunge, making it as extreme as you can without losing control of your body.
   2. Get contact on his thigh (high up on your shoulder with your ear grazing the side of his leg, and with your head up) and simultaneously with this contact, have your legs up under your body (not stretched out behind) and on a broad stance.
   3. Work from underneath with a lifting action slipping your shoulder toward his waist and with your legs driving like pistons with high knee action and continuing on a broad base.
   4. If opponent is slipping or overpowering you, work your legs in the direction he is fighting too, (otherwise you will lose him). If your shoulder has slipped off by the side of him, move the leg closest to him across in front of him locking him in and continue to drive him with your side.

2. Double shoulder block
   If the intention is to ride your opponent back, everything is exactly the same as single shoulder block. If the idea is to ride him to the left the blocker on the left after contact just drives hard enough to hold that contact while the blocker on the right drives opponent to the left.

3. Side block
   a. Used as a follow up if shoulder block misses or intentionally used when you want to hold a defensive man in position.
   All preliminary points are exactly the same as in the shoulder block. The only difference is this: Instead of hitting the thigh with the shoulder, you let the shoulder slip by bringing the inside leg across in front of opponents body, and apply as much pressure as possible with the side, and continuing to drive the legs to keep the pressure on. (Do not merely throw your body across in front of the opponent with the hope that he may move into the trap, most of the time he won't, you must go after him with the same aggressiveness you would or should use in a shoulder block)

Keep on your feet:
4. Check block
   There are varying degrees used where opponents (1) must be held into position for a short time, or, (2) where it is only necessary to slow up his charge.
   In (1) put on a side block and then release to continue on another assignment.
   In (2) drive your shoulder into him unbalancing him or slowing him down and then continue on your other assignment.
5. Fill in block
   Used where the following situations occur.

   3 must side block defensive man 2 is pulling out and 1 ultimate assignment is as a downfield blocker. If 1 busts out with 2 alongside of him pulling out defensive man has a big gap to charge thru so 1 steps in the direction of 2 acting as a buffer until 3 applies his block.

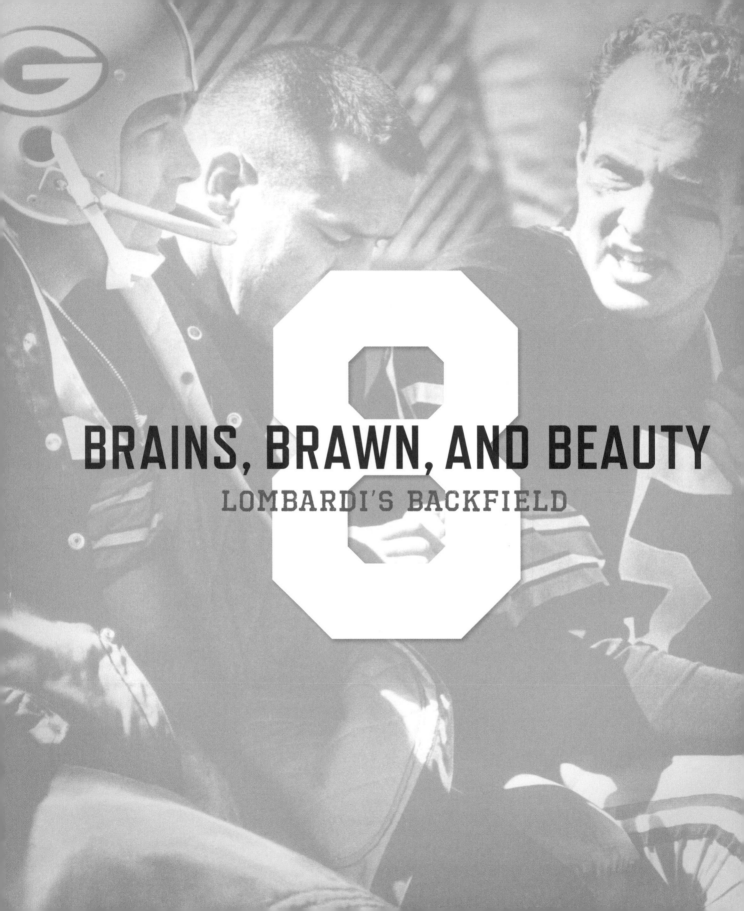

BRAINS, BRAWN, AND BEAUTY

LOMBARDI'S BACKFIELD

Bart Starr accepts the snap from his center and takes that first step backward. Freeze the image. At this point, one of three things is likely to happen. Starr can pivot one way and hand the ball to fullback Jim Taylor. He can turn in the opposite direction and give it to halfback Paul Hornung. Or he can continue to drop back and rely on his own passing.

How could the Packers go wrong with three Hall of Fame options?

Taylor was one of the most punishing runners in NFL history, the only man ever to wrest the league rushing title from the incomparable Jim Brown. Hornung was a master of versatility with a nose for the end zone (and for cold drinks and beautiful women). Starr was the ultimate game manager and an unshakable big-game quarterback. All three have bronze likenesses at the Pro Football Hall of Fame in Canton.

In Hornung, Lombardi had the good fortune to find the Midwest equivalent of Frank Gifford, the star of his New York Giants' offense. Gifford could run, catch the ball and—key to keeping defenses honest—throw it accurately, too.

When Lombardi joined the Giants staff in 1954, the halfback option play was one of the first things he installed. His Army team had played USC in the mud at Yankee Stadium, and he remembered how Gifford had hurt the Black Knights not just with his running but with his passing. So Lombardi

began to flank his right halfback wide and send his fullback forward to block, successfully adapting a Single-Wing play to the T-formation.

When Lombardi got to Green Bay, he broke down the Packers' film from the previous year and decided that Hornung could be his new Gifford. Hornung had won the Heisman Trophy at Notre Dame, but hadn't hit his stride while bouncing around the backfield during his first two seasons in Green Bay.

Lombardi phoned him immediately and made it clear: Hornung would be the Packers' starting halfback. "Before Lombardi arrived, I was a jumping jack," Hornung said, as quoted in a May 1963 edition of *Current Biography*. "Once I was a quarterback, then a fullback. I never knew where I might end up. When he came, everything changed. He said, 'You're going to be my left halfback, period.' Having a coach's backing was like coming out of the dark."

OPPOSITE Bart Starr, Jim Taylor, and Paul Hornung on the Packers' bench. All three are in the Pro Football Hall of Fame. **ABOVE** The burly Taylor follows a block by Forrest Gregg in Super Bowl I.

89

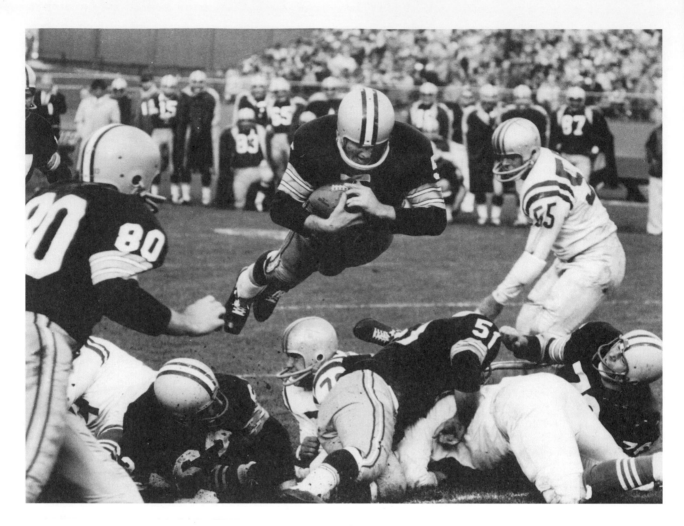

Like Gifford before him, Hornung wasn't particularly big or fast. But he was shifty and tough, and he seemed to have an innate feel for running in traffic—especially near the end zone. "I have heard and read that Paul Hornung is not a great runner or a great passer or a great field-goal kicker, but he led the league in scoring for three seasons," Lombardi wrote in *Run to Daylight*, the book he did with W.C. Heinz. "What it comes down to is that in the middle of the field he may be only slightly better than an average ballplayer, but inside the twenty-yard line he is one of the greatest I've ever seen. He smells that goal line."

Hornung scored 33 points in one game against Baltimore in 1961, a mark eclipsed by only three NFL players. He tallied a total of 176 points in 1960, a record that stood for 46 years, until San Diego's LaDainian Tomlinson scored 186.

Perhaps more important than his ability to throw the deep ball or sniff out the end zone, however, was Hornung's role as buffer. Lombardi would shower his party-hearty halfback with verbal abuse on the practice field and sidelines, and Hornung would stoically take it, allowing some of his teammates to momentarily escape the thunderstorm. But underneath it all, Lombardi loved Hornung as a player and seemed to be hugely fond of him as a man, even as the halfback stayed out half the night. Hornung certainly understood that the old man's anger was at least partly theater for the benefit of the other players.

ABOVE Hornung soars into the end zone for a touchdown against the 49ers in 1960, the year he scored 176 points.

Taylor was a much different character. He wasn't nearly as gregarious as Hornung, nor as imperturbable. He could be prickly with teammates, and Lombardi gave him a longer leash. On the field, though, no one put out more effort than the fullback from Baton Rouge, Louisiana—Taylor was way ahead of his time when it came to conditioning. He worked out year-round, and was a solid block of muscle. It was no doubt one of the reasons he proved so durable. While Hornung's offensive statistics fall far short of his reputation, Taylor's are superlative: five 1,000-yard rushing seasons and a career total of 8,597 yards on the ground.

Taylor and Hornung weren't the Packers' only running backs, of course. Lombardi had solid backups in guys like Tom Moore, Elijah Pitts, Donny Anderson and Jim Grabowski. All of them had important moments, all of them fit nicely into the Green Bay offensive package.

But when Taylor bolted for New Orleans in 1967, and Hornung soon followed—plucked by the Saints in the expansion draft—it was clear the team would never have a one-two punch to match the original. "All the backs were good at following [on the power sweep], but none as good as Hornung," former guard Jerry Kramer says. "He wasn't a speed burner, and maybe that's part of the reason, too—he was so aware. Pitts would come into a game later on, and we'd get on the corner, and Elijah would run right by us. He just didn't have the patience and maturity to wait. . . . It took him two or three years for him to let things open up instead of running wildly by us."

The third position in the Packers' backfield escaped such turnover during Lombardi's era. Bart Starr was in Green Bay before the coach arrived, and he was still starting for the Packers when Lombardi died in 1970.

Lombardi had a fine quarterback in New York (the poised, courageous Charlie Conerly) and another later in Washington (Sonny Jurgensen, one of the finest pure passers ever). But rarely have a coach and quarterback been more inextricably linked than Lombardi and Starr, who proved to be the perfect instrument of the coach's grand plans. Starr was a cool and reliable field general quite willing to subjugate his ego if it helped his team win.

"Of all the people on your ball club—and you are involved with all of them—there is no other with whom you spend as much time as you do with your quarterback," the coach said, as quoted by his son, Vince Jr., in *The Essential Vince Lombardi.* "If this is a game through which you find self-expression—and if it isn't, you don't belong in it—then that quarterback is the primary extension of yourself and is your greatest challenge."

Lombardi kept 4-by-6 index cards with the heading "Q.B. Strategy," which include a list of his "4 main characteristics" of a quarterback: qualities like common sense, leadership, and grace under pressure. Notice that he says nothing of heaving the ball 60 yards or throwing an out pass with precision. Lombardi clearly believed a quarterback's most important traits were intangible, and in these Starr had no equal.

ABOVE Taylor goes head-to-head with Larry Wilson, the great Cardinals safety.

91

In *Lombardi on Football*, the coach offers a longer description of his ideal QB: ". . . a quarterback must have sure hands and be an excellent passer. His I.Q. must be above average. . . . The quarterback should be strong physically and be able to take the punishment when those 270-pounders unload on him. He should also have enough height to see his receivers over those opposing linemen. . . . A quarterback should have great poise, too, and he must not be panicked by what the defense does or what his own offense fails to do."

It sounds like Superman, though Bart Starr hardly looked or behaved like a superhero. He excelled in Lombardi's system because he knew his place in the chain of command—Starr came from a military family—and because he had a quiet inner toughness. "Bart was first of all a fine person, a man of character—and I'll probably go ahead and say a man of faith," says former receiver Carroll Dale. "He had priorities, and his God or religion came first, his family second and the Green Bay Packers third—which was Coach Lombardi's speech every training camp."

It's easy to forget that it took a while for Starr and Lombardi to mesh, though it shouldn't be surprising when you consider their opposite personalities. Starr got an inkling of what was in store for him when he first saw a photo of the Packers' new coach in one of the Green Bay newspapers in 1959. He immediately recalled Lombardi from a preseason game against New York the year before, at Fenway Park in Boston.

"While jogging off after holding for the extra point and going past the Giants' bench, I see this guy who is ranting and raving at defensive players for the Giants," Starr told Chuck Carlson in *Game of My Life: Green Bay Packers*. "Then I recognized him. To show you his aggressiveness and intensity, he was yelling at the defensive players and he was the offensive line coach."

Their relationship was rocky at first. The salient moment occurred during the 1959 season, when Lombardi verbally dressed down Starr on the practice field. He did that to everybody, of course, but Starr wouldn't have it. He visited the

Q.B. STRATEGY

Bart Starr's reputation as a product of Lombardi's offense—even an automaton—was unfair. Starr was a superb play caller and a charismatic field commander. He also had the ability to throw for 300 yards if the defense loaded up against the run.

Lombardi definitely was a control freak when it came to his quarterbacks, though. He had specific instructions on every part of their technique, whether it was dropping back and setting up in the pocket, arm motion, looking for receivers, handing off, or taking off and running. He also had explicit notions of what to do in certain downs-and-distances, and would rehearse them with Starr each week.

These index cards on quarterback strategy (here and following page) demonstrate Lombardi's attention to detail. They also illustrate how important he believed the position to be.

In these notes you see the tightrope the coach walked between conservatism and risk-taking on the field. On card #3, he explains how his strategy is affected by the score: If you're up by eight points, "be careful"; if you're down by three or five or eight, there's "no hurry." And while advocating an element of surprise on card #2, Lombardi sought to clarify by adding in longhand: "Surprize not radical breaking."

Q.B. Strategy

I. Many theories as to stance, position
  A. Ours not only way
  B Our system of off nse
2. Positive ideas as to A. position B. Q.B. exch nge
3. Stance
    feet, body, distance, hands
4. C & Q.B. exchange
    diff. - split T
5. Pivots. Straight; reverse
6. Hand off position of feet
7. Faking, inside belly for instance
8. Back to pass
    passes out of run
    roll outs
    drop back a. straight back b. half turn
        show pass; fake pass, draw, screen etc

① Range T. Pass -

Delivery.

Q.B. Strategy # 2

9. Books on strat. many do's and dont's
10. Imp. of Q.B.; mental ability, common sense
11. 4 main characteristics
    1. think under pressure
    2. transmit common sense to teammates
    3. qualities of leadership
    4. talent think thru things able to reason, not
        reckless gambling. Ctp is enrol.
12. signal in huddle
13. set change up, cadence
14. change up, most imp. strat.
    plays against defense
15. off. patern against major defense
    multiple defenses e.g.
16. change up system — simple High School
17. 2 teams evenly matched, def. -fooled, outmanuevered
    surprized, keep opponents guessing
18. Element of surprise 1. rapidity of manuever 2 deception

Surprze not reckled Breaking

Q.B. strat. # 3

Strat. depends upon circumstance
   1 Score 8
         8 be careful
         6-7 gamble
         12-16 get another
   behind 123-678 no hurry
         12- 16 shoot works
   2 Time
   3 position
   4 down and distance
   5 weather
      The specific play under one of above is
determined by one of following

Q.B. Strat. #4
Running game

1. know strongest blockers,use short yds
2 run at tired or dazed defenders
3 run at weak link on plats of imp.
4. dont depend on making 10 yds consistently thru the
     line-if evenly matched the ball will be lost
     after several first downs
5. Best play best ball carrier on first down ydage
6. 2and short still best poss. sit.
7. stick to run. game if good, dont switch , sake of sw.
8. inside and outside
9 dont be patterned to down and pos.
10. Make them defense your best play

coach in his office and calmly but sternly told him, "If you want me to be the leader of this team, you can't undermine me in front of the other players. Whatever you have to say to me, do it privately."

Lombardi never again barked at Starr in earshot of the troops, at least not in a serious way. But the coach did lecture his quarterback, constantly and repetitively, as evidenced by the Q.B. Strategy index cards' outline of techniques—Stance, Pivots, etc.—and guides to use of the running game and passing game. Perhaps most interesting is how Lombardi's strategies shift depending on the score of a game ("Strat. depends upon circumstance").

Lombardi had a vast body of advice for his quarterbacks, everything from the proper dropback technique to how to cope with bad weather. But a lot of what he preached fell into one basic category: Don't take unnecessary chances with

the ball. Vince Jr. quotes his father as saying: "The mark of a great quarterback is the ability to stay away from stupid calls. The gambling quarterback disappears fast."

"His main purpose was to maintain possession of the ball and score points," Dale says. "He'd go bananas if the quarterback threw into double coverage. He'd always say, no matter how good you are, two men have an advantage on one."

Lombardi's quarterbacks—primarily Starr, of course—had to tread a fine line when they were pressured. The old man would go ballistic if they threw the ball up for grabs, but they were also expected to avoid sacks if possible. Ideally, they'd throw the ball away and forfeit one down.

"It's also quite an art to be able to throw that ball in an area where it can't be caught by either your receiver or their defender," the coach says in *Lombardi on Football*. "Many of the great quarterbacks have mastered that art and I remember

ABOVE Starr (15) demanded Lombardi's outward respect. In return, he became a loyal on-field extension of the coach.

95

seeing Bart Starr one time put it right into the tuba section of the Packers' band on the sidelines and defense screamed that it was intentional grounding, but there was a receiver nearby and the referee didn't call it."

Starr excelled at these subtle aspects of game management, and he was a highly accurate short- to mid-range passer. But what truly made him a Hall of Famer was his play calling. Lombardi would go over the game plan with Starr during the week and narrow the focus to 15-20 basic play sets. They always had specific contingencies for various situations. "We were coached, in a sense, by down and distance," backup quarterback Zeke Bratkowski notes. "He said, 'On third-and-11 these are your choices,' and you'd call one of 'em."

Once the game started, Lombardi turned it over to Starr. Pretty much all NFL quarterbacks called their own plays in those days, but Starr had a knack for it. "The things that made him so good weren't the things you saw in the paper the next day," says former receiver Boyd Dowler, who played with Starr for eleven seasons. "Calling plays is not an easy thing to do. But he always seemed to call the right play. He's as close to being the reason we did what we did as anyone on the team."

For an illustration of Starr's genius, Dowler points to the Ice Bowl, the infamous 1967 NFL Championship Game against Dallas. The receiver mentions four specific play calls that he believes decided the Packers' 21–17 victory. One was a fake weakside slant to the fullback, followed by a pass into the wind to Dowler, which went for a second-quarter touchdown. Another was the sucker play to fullback Chuck Mercein on Green Bay's clinching drive. Another was the final touchdown, Starr's dive on a wedge play called for Mercein.

All of them were perfect choices, all of them hatched by Starr. But the one that still awes Dowler, and perhaps the least remembered, was the Packers' first touchdown. It was in the first quarter of a scoreless game, and Green Bay was on the Cowboys' 8-yard line. In the huddle, Starr called a play that brought Dowler in tight on the left—basically a weakside tight end. But at the line, the quarterback audibled to a pass called 86.

"For the life of me, I never ran 86 Audible from weakside tight end," Dowler says. "We'd never even discussed it. I had my head between my legs, thinking, 'What does he want me to do?' Well, the linebacker was outside me, the safety was by the line of scrimmage, the cornerback was playing me outside. All I had to do was plant my foot and break into the middle, and we had a touchdown. It looked like we'd run it warming up before the game, but we'd never even practiced it." Somehow, in a matter of seconds, Starr had read the defense, discovered a weakness and adapted a play to beat it.

It wasn't the only time the Packers had success with a play change. Lombardi's code for audibles was to repeat the snap-count number. If the call in the huddle was "49 on 3," then "3" became the quarterback's signal to listen for an audible. If he barked out "3 . . . 29 . . . " then everyone knew 29 was the new play. "Every play versus a defense that we had in the running game, we could get out of it and get to a better play," Bratkowski says. "His concept was, don't go from a good run and try to find a better one. Let the good run go. But if it's against a [disadvantageous] defense, get out of it and go to this one."

And it usually started with Starr. He didn't amaze people with his arm, which is one reason he played five seasons before truly distinguishing himself. But finally given an opportunity to run a team, and a coach who knew him inside and out, Starr blossomed into one of the NFL's biggest winners ever.

"They said he couldn't throw well enough and wasn't tough enough, that he had no confidence in himself and that no one had confidence in him," Lombardi told Flynn. "But after looking at those films over and over before the first team meeting, I knew he had the ability, the arm, the ball-handling techniques and the intelligence, but what I didn't know was what kind of inner strength he had and how much confidence he had. He proved that to me and to all of football."

ABOVE Starr was as tough as they came under pressure. Here he unloads before getting decked by a Detroit Lions lineman in 1969.

HIRED HANDS
LOMBARDI'S RECEIVERS

Lombardi had a genius for analyzing his players' individual personalities and finding ways to extract the most out of them. You have to wonder how he'd fare with the wide receivers of the new millennium.

Keyshawn Johnson, now retired, wrote a book called *Just Give Me the Damn Ball!*, in which he disparaged teammate and fellow receiver Wayne Chrebet. Terrell Owens, currently with Dallas, exploded at least two offenses when he felt he wasn't being used properly. And even Jerry Rice, generally considered the greatest (and perhaps hardest-working) pass catcher ever, threw his helmet to the ground in anger when his streak of consecutive games with a reception ended—when he might have been celebrating a much-needed win for his Oakland Raiders.

Imagine how these divas would have reacted to Lombardi's offensive scheme.

"It was all based on the running game," former split end Boyd Dowler says. "You had to understand that if you got thrown five balls per game, you'd better end up catching three. And if you had ten thrown your way, you'd better catch six or seven. I led the team in receiving a lot of years [seven], but the most I caught was fifty-four."

Lombardi's reliance upon the run affected Bart Starr's reputation, too, tempering his production and causing some

to view him as a mere cog in the Green Bay machine. But a quarterback's ultimate legacy is tied closely to winning, and the Packers did plenty of that. Anyway, Starr could point to sky-high completion percentages and low interception rates.

Lombardi's receivers had no such supporting evidence. Their worth is largely judged on raw numbers, and these were modest. Dowler's 54 catches in 1967, Lombardi's final season as Packers coach, were the most anyone got during his nine years in Wisconsin. Dowler led the 1959 team with a mere 32 receptions. Lombardi never had a 1,000-yard receiver, and that includes his stints with the Giants and Redskins. But make no mistake; the Titletown Packers had some excellent receivers.

Dowler and Max McGee were fixtures at wide receiver for Lombardi's first six seasons in Green Bay. The coach traded for the fleet Carroll Dale in 1965, and he immediately stretched the field from the flanker position. Meanwhile,

OPPOSITE Max McGee makes a catch against the Colts in 1958, the year before Lombardi arrived in Green Bay. **ABOVE** Boyd Dowler's presence on the team convinced Lombardi to add a full-time flanker to his starting lineup in 1959.

99

Lombardi's tight ends were ahead of their time in terms of receiving ability. That was Gary Knafelc for a couple years, Ron Kramer for four and Marv Fleming for three.

Dowler and McGee—and to some extent the tight ends, too—were fairly interchangeable, and that was by design. If the quarterback audibled to a different play in Lombardi's system, no one would motion to a new position. Rather, the ends would simply change roles. Sometimes the tight end would widen his placement and become a split end, while the split end on the opposite side would move to the tackle's shoulder and become a blocker.

So Lombardi's receivers tended to be big and physical. Dowler was 6' 5", 224 pounds. McGee was 6' 3", 205. Kramer was 6' 3", 234. Fleming was 6' 4", 232. Even Dale, more of a traditional flanker, was a solid 6' 2", 200. Lombardi knew they weren't track stars. But he fully expected them to run precise routes, catch the ball when it was thrown to them, and block effectively, if not overpoweringly.

ABOVE Dowler holds on for a touchdown as he is upended by Dallas safety Mike Gaechter in the 1966 NFL title game.

"We were good on third down. We all had size, and we worked the middle of the field very well," Dowler says. "We got in the middle, found holes and competed for the ball. Our whole passing game was based on: Read the defense, get to where you belong and watch the quarterback."

Because the personnel remained fairly constant, the Green Bay receivers wound up having almost telepathic bonds with Starr, their heady quarterback. He was apt at spotting mismatches, and it got to the point where a receiver could usually tell if the ball was headed his way as soon as he saw the defensive alignment. "If it was man coverage, you were responsible to beat that man," Dowler says. "You'd better use your eyes and understand what he's doing. If he lines up inside, he probably doesn't have help inside. Go beat him. Even if you had an inside route called, there are ways to get inside against coverage."

Dowler was Mr. Consistent for the Packers. McGee, on the other hand, was a free spirit like his good friend and carousing partner, Paul Hornung. He was the class clown of the practice field, one of the few players who could get away with cracking wise in Lombardi's presence—largely because the coach felt McGee couldn't handle criticism. McGee did just enough to get by in practice, but was a reliable game-day performer. He stayed out all night on the eve of Super Bowl I, figuring he wouldn't play. When Dowler re-injured his shoulder on the first series, McGee, pressed into bleary-eyed service, made seven receptions for 138 yards and two touchdowns.

"If Max were a perfectionist, there's no telling how great a receiver he might be," Lombardi once said, as quoted by Vince Jr. in *The Essential Vince Lombardi*. "But then, pressing all the time as perfectionists must, he would probably lose one of his greatest assets, his ability to relax. He can relax before, during, and after a game, and it makes him a great clutch player, although it also contributes to his tendency to be a little careless."

It's remarkable to hear the unyielding coach describe a player in such forgiving terms. Less surprising is that

Lombardi would have plenty to say about playing receiver, a position he supposedly undervalued.

His notes include a long treatise headed THE MULTIPLE USE OF FLANKERS (next three pages), which he apparently used while speaking at a football clinic on the subject while he was an assistant in New York. In his introduction, Lombardi defends the use of the flanker attack against criticisms, arguing that the formation can actually generate a better balance between running and passing.

Lombardi then lists specific advantages to the flanker attack, building his case, and goes on to present the various defenses an NFL team might employ to stop a flanker-based offensive set, complete with diagrams—and then sets about picking apart those defenses.

In *Lombardi on Football*, he also offers some detailed coaching points on a receiver's crack-back block—wherein the end

ABOVE After staying out most of the night, McGee was a surprise star in Super Bowl I, with 138 yards and two touchdowns.

101

THE MULTIPLE USE OF FLANKERS

I. INTRODUCTION

The flanker attack has many good points.However there are many who have objectd to this type of attack or formation. The largest criticismn seems to be that the attack lacks balance.

We believe we have balance and can generate a better balance betwween running and passing. This I believe is of great importance espec ly so if your meterial and opposition necessitate the changing of your pattern from week to week, from either a running concentration to a passing concentration or vice versa.

I dont believe anyone questions the fact that a flanker makes a greater passing game possible. Thus if a balanced running attack can be developed(this by the way is what I shall concentrate on, since I know you are to receive a lecture on the pass later)-- we can concentrate either way.

II. ADVANTAGES

There are many advantages to the flanker attack.

1. We can place anyone of our backs against any one particular defender

2. We can set our three best receivers to one side or the other

3. Another possibility is to always use your best receiver and blocker as a flanker and keep ypur best two running backs in.

4. Able to get three men deep on passes unless they compensate. If they do, it eliminates the nine man front so popular today and so dif difficult to run against.

5.A very strong attack to the to the flanker side- for which they must compensate by rolling the backs or overshifting the linebackers or the line.

6. By splitting an end and setting a flanker to the opposite side, we believe we can force one of the defenders to play a very large zone.

7. The basic idea is to force the defense to compensate, so that basic plays can be run to the weakness

LLI. FLANKER POSITIONS

Close ; Near; and Far ＋ INSIDE

When used

IV. FLANKER SET UP AND TERMINOLOGY

Bal. Rt.; Bal. Rt Over; Bal. Rt Inside (over)

St. Rt.; St. Rt. over; St rt Inside(over)

Split the opposite end with the above.

Repeat Questions From Audience

V. Defenses for the flanker
    1. Roll the backs to place a second man outside the defensive end.

        Feel Imust mention the passing possibilities slightly for you to gte abetter picture of what we are trying to accomplish
    1.1 on 1 situation
    2.possibility of forcing end or linebacker to cover a fast H.B.
    3. If end drops off to cover(a) force him to play run(b) fake run and pass © *fake pass + run*
    4. Certain types of zone passes into strength
        Must defense floods and rollouts
    5. Defense still the same from end to end -
    6. Definate weakness for run to weakside - *9 MAN FRONT*

  II. Balanced Defense
    1.cover near back back with linebacker
    2.move into roll on snap of ball
    3. overshift line or angle

    1. Type of pass used to combat roll on snap
    2.Burden on weak side safety and H.B.
    # check above
III. Split end away from flanker

    1. In coordination with first or second defense
    2.Like to work on weak side linebacker
with swing passes
    ③ *Swing Passes*

I

In coordination with the flanker I shall try to ~~go into as~~
~~many of these as~~ 2 or 3 series and some of the basic plays from each

The balanced defense V.S. the split 'T'

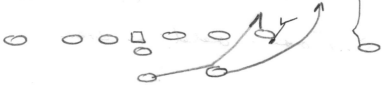

1. Option play now to the F.B. with plenty of lead blockers
2. Line blocking same as without a flanker
3. Near H.B. flares as the F.B. would and is lead blocker
4. Q.B. pattern is the same
5. Flanker watches defensive end; if he crosses line of scrimmage
go down for safety; if end holds he blocks accordingly.

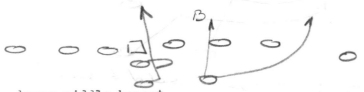

1. In the off tackle hole we use the same basic play with only
one change in assignment, the near H.B.
2. Forces the end to play tight in the offtackle hole; also a
good strong play against the sliding line by allowing the F.B. to
run to daylight.
3. Line blocking the same , must keep constant pressure in any
direction.

1. Co. play - keeps middle honest
2. Near back either flares or dives depending on play of linebacker

1. The handoff speaks for itself, still the basic play, the play
the defense must always be geared to stop.
2. The split 'T' Co. to take care of overshift or the key of
the linebacker

The passing possibilities using the fake run and pass and
from the flanker set up s are many and fairrly obvious

sneaks in from a wide position to block a linebacker from the side and seal the edge on an outside running play:

"In any crack-back block, whether it be from the flanker or the X end, the first step is not at the man he's going to crack down on but rather flat down the line of scrimmage. And the reason is that if the defensive man were to come across quickly to meet the play, the crack-back blocker is in position to take him. . . . If he comes down flat and defensive linebacker stays where he is, the blocker can always turn and go upfield to get him."

If Lombardi's wide receivers were valuable contributors, his tight ends did more to establish his impact on the game. Before 1959, most NFL teams lined up with a pair of split ends and a flanker. "Lombardi had a strong-side end, a blocking end, and that's where the term 'tight end' came from," Knafelc told Gary D'Amato in *Stadium Stories: Green Bay Packers*. "The Bears used to have a slot back, but there was really no designated tight end until Lombardi."

Today, the situation has sort of swung back to the extreme, with most high-profile tight ends little more than oversized wide receivers (despite where they line up). In Lombardi's offense, the tight end was a true two-way threat, an extra lineman on running plays or an extra receiver on pass plays. In fact, Lombardi once wrote that Kramer was like a twelfth man on the field because of his dual role. "It was probably the greatest compliment he could pay to anybody," Kramer says proudly.

Kramer's blocking against the Giants' Sam Huff in the 1961 NFL Championship Game was one of the keys to the Packers' 37–0 victory. "Sam Huff, a good, if no longer great, middle linebacker, was surprised several times when Kramer, a massive and agile offensive end, came across to hit Huff after [center Jim] Ringo had brushed him with a soft block as the play developed," Tex Maule wrote in a *Sports Illustrated* account. "This prevented Huff from swinging wide against the Green Bay off-tackle plays to the strong side. From the observable violence of the blocks by Kramer, it must also have bruised him painfully."

And the tight end's block was crucial on the power sweep, that iconic Packers play. The goal was to isolate the tight end (or, as Lombardi often called him, the Y end) and the outside linebacker on that side, as detailed in *Lombardi on Football*, "so that the ball carrier can either cut inside the block of the Y end or outside of that block." Kramer was good enough to take on the linebacker by himself, freeing up another blocker to hit someone else.

But when called upon, Kramer and his successor, Fleming, were important targets for Starr in the passing game. They just couldn't expect the numbers of contemporaries like Mike Ditka in Chicago or John Mackey in Baltimore.

"We had some great pass-catching ends, only because they threw so few to us," Kramer says, echoing Dowler's sentiments. "You had to catch everything thrown to you."

ABOVE Ron Kramer, shown here in a 1963 game at St. Louis, was one of the NFL's first modern tight ends.

10 REACHING THE PINNACLE
THE EARLY CHAMPIONSHIPS

It would be hard to imagine a less promising situation than the one Lombardi encountered in Green Bay in 1959. The Packers had a running streak of eleven consecutive years without a winning record, punctuated by an embarrassing 1-10-1 mark in 1958. The coach that season had been Ray (Scooter) McLean, a kind, popular man who seemed unwilling or unable to discipline his players. "The Packers were the most soft-bitten team in the league," wrote *New York Herald-Tribune* scribe Red Smith, a Green Bay native. "They overwhelmed one, underwhelmed ten, and whelmed one."

Lombardi broke down film of the '58 season and concluded the team had some talent, despite its record. And Green Bay offered a loyally rabid fan base. His challenge was to change the culture of losing. "Our number-one problem here is to defeat defeatism," is how Lombardi put it.

Appearing before the Packers' 45 directors—the team was, and is, the only one in the NFL with public ownership—for the first time in February, 1959, the new coach didn't mince words. "I want it understood that I'm in complete command," he said. "I expect full cooperation from you people, and you will get full cooperation from me in return." Desperate for success, the board acquiesced.

And make no mistake, Lombardi was in charge. He ordered that the nameplate on his door read "Mr. Lombardi" rather than "Coach Lombardi." He controlled matters as important as player personnel transactions, and as seemingly trivial as uniform design; he changed the jersey and pants upon arrival (they were nearly identical to those worn by the Packers today), and instructed equipment man Dad Braisher to add the iconic "G" to the helmets in 1961. When he dictated memos to a secretary, he meticulously included all punctuation.

The players quickly discovered the days of country-club atmosphere were gone. Lombardi instituted strict guidelines for comportment—coats and ties for travel, no standing at bars while drinking, etc.—and set the clocks to what would be known as Lombardi Time. You were expected to be ten

---

OPPOSITE Lombardi brought a feeling of industry and confidence when he was hired to coach the downtrodden Packers in 1959. **ABOVE** The coach at training camp at St. Norbert College, where he began to mold losers into winners.

THE STATE OF WISCONSIN

CERTIFICATE OF CONGRATULATIONS

Whereas, THE GREEN BAY PACKERS FOOTBALL TEAM

has HAD OUTSTANDING SUCCESS IN THE PAST;

Now, therefore, pursuant to Joint Rule 26 upon the motion of SENATOR O'BRIEN **and** ASSEMBLYMAN LEONARD, **the legislature extends to** VINCE LOMBARDI, MANAGER OF THE TEAM, **their most sincere congratulations upon** THE SUCCESS OF THE TEAM IN THE PAST AND EXPRESSES THE WISH THAT THEIR PAST SUCCESSES MAY CONTINUE IN THE FUTURE **and direct that this certificate of congratulations be presented to** MR. VINCE LOMBARDI .

Philip Nsh
Lieutenant Governor

Laurence R Larsen
Chief Clerk

George Molinaro
Speaker of the Assembly

august 27, 1959.
Date

ABOVE No pressure to win . . . just a certificate from the Wisconsin state legislature wishing the new coach future success.

minutes early to practices, meals, and meetings, and they would begin precisely when they scheduled to begin. Curfew was 11 p.m. during training camp, and violators would be fined. "I believe a man should be on time—not a minute late, not ten seconds late—but on time for things," Lombardi told *Sports Illustrated* in 1969. "I believe that a man who's late for meetings or for the bus won't run his pass routes right. He'll be sloppy."

His demands were not merely mental. He worked his players like mules at training camp at St. Norbert College in DePere that summer, and would continue to do so during his tenure in Green Bay. "The harder a man works, the harder it is to surrender, and that's why you're going to work like you've never worked before in these next days, weeks, and months," the coach told his troops. "That's why I'm going to push you until I know you're doing your best. If you can't take it, get out."

"He said, 'There are planes, trains, and buses leaving every day,'" remembers former defensive end Jim Temp. "He instilled the fear of God in you."

Tight end Gary Knafelc once remarked, "Coach Lombardi works you so hard that when he tells you to go to hell, you look forward to the trip."

And few of the players rebelled. They were intimidated, sure. But they also were aching to be winners, and they sensed Lombardi was their vehicle.

Always an astute judge of talent, Lombardi immediately orchestrated some important trades. He got a pair of defensive linemen, Henry Jordan and Bill Quinlan, from Cleveland in exchange for wide receiver Billy Howton. He picked up Pro Bowl safety Emlen Tunnell from the Giants, guard Fuzzy Thurston from the Colts, and quarterback Lamar McHan from the Cardinals. And he replaced Howton by drafting Boyd Dowler, a quarterback from Colorado whom he would convert to receiver.

Most of the men who would start for Lombardi in 1959, however, were leftovers from the dismal '58 team. They included tackle Forrest Gregg, halfback Paul Hornung,

guard Jerry Kramer, wide receiver Max McGee, middle linebacker Ray Nitschke, center Jim Ringo, quarterback Bart Starr, and fullback Jim Taylor—the backbone of the upcoming championship teams. It may be the greatest testimony to Lombardi that he was able to recognize and realize the potential of players who were little more than average before he arrived. Eleven players from the 1958 1-10-1 team went on to be All-Pro.

The results were swift. In the opening game of the season on September 27, the Packers surprised the Chicago Bears, who had finished 8-4 in 1958 and would do so again in 1959, by winning 9–6. The players spontaneously carried Lombardi from the field on their shoulders, the first of at least five times that would happen.

Green Bay delighted its fans by jumping to a 3-0 start, then proceeded to lose five in a row. Lombardi kept the ship

ABOVE Lombardi was not well known by the general public when he came to Green Bay, but that would change quickly.

109

steady. "We lost five in a row, but he didn't really go ballistic," Dowler remembers. "He was a pretty volatile guy, but he wasn't throwing his arms up. His main move was, I began to start. He didn't change the offense, didn't get depressed. He saw we were gonna be pretty good."

Lombardi scrapped his three-back set, common at the time, and began to use two wide receivers—Dowler and McGee—and a tight end on most plays. The Packers recovered to win the final four games (by then, Starr had replaced McHan at quarterback) and finish at a respectable 7-5, tied for third in the Western Conference. Lombardi, the rookie field general, was voted NFL coach of the year.

Packers fans may not have known it, but the 1959 season could have been Lombardi's last in Green Bay. Jim Lee Howell announced that he would be the Giants' head coach for only one more year, and team owner Wellington Mara, a college classmate at Fordham, targeted Lombardi, also an ex-employee, as his replacement. A return to the East Coast would have appealed greatly to Vince Lombardi, and even more to Marie, but the two sides agreed to table the matter until after the 1960 season, in deference to Lombardi's commitment to the Packers.

The 1960 campaign did much to cement Lombardi as the man in Green Bay. He bolstered his defense before the

ABOVE A victorious Lombardi leaves the field in Green Bay after his first game, a 9–6 upset of the hated Bears.

season by trading for Cleveland defensive end Willie Davis and signing unheralded free-agent safety Willie Wood; both would end up in the Hall of Fame. The Packers, in the mix at 5-4 after nine games, won their last three on the road to edge Detroit and San Francisco for the Western Conference title. They hadn't won a division/conference title since 1944, and their fans were delirious.

Their foes in the 1960 NFL Championship Game were the Philadelphia Eagles, surprise winners who rode the arm of thirty-four-year-old quarterback Norm Van Brocklin and the fire of thirty-five-year-old center/linebacker Chuck Bednarik. Bednarik had begun the season as a center, then accepted double duty when the Eagles' suffered injuries at linebacker. He has been known ever since as the last of the 60-minute men.

The Packers probably had the better team that day at Philadelphia's Franklin Field. But trips to the Eagles' 5-, 13-, 8- and 7-yard lines netted only two field goals, and Green Bay lost 17–13. The outcome was in doubt until the final play, when Taylor caught a pass from Starr and rumbled to the Eagles' 9-yard line. There, Bednarik pounced on Taylor and lay on him until the gun sounded. "You can get up now," the linebacker snarled. "You just lost."

Trivia answer: Buck Shaw was the only coach ever to beat Lombardi in a postseason game. Lombardi would never lose another. "We thought we were ready and would win, but we weren't and we got beat," he would reflect later, after he owned five NFL championships. "All of us have regretted that ever since. We have never forgotten it. We don't talk about it much, but it's always in the back of our minds."

Though sorely disappointed, Lombardi and his Packers began the 1961 season brimming with confidence. They had come within nine yards of a title, and believed their best days were ahead. The Packers' executive committee kept the coach from bolting to New York by offering him a new five-year contract that pushed his salary above $50,000.

After losing to Detroit in the first game of 1961, the Packers ripped off four convincing victories, capped by a 49–17

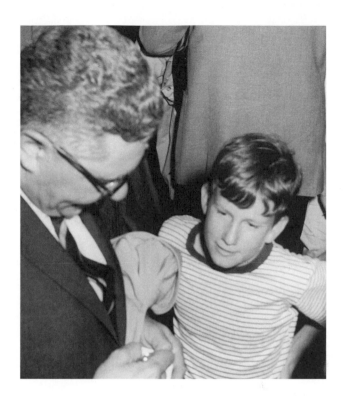

win at Cleveland. Then the U.S. government threw Lombardi a curveball. In response to the Soviets' construction of the Berlin Wall, President John F. Kennedy (who had already become a Lombardi booster) activated thousands of members of the military reserves and national guards. Among the reservists were three of the Packers' best players—Hornung, Nitschke, and Dowler.

As documented by David Maraniss in *When Pride Still Mattered*, Lombardi sent a personal note to Pentagon officials pleading to defer the service of Hornung and Nitschke. When it was denied by an Army panel, the two players filed individual appeals. Those, too, were rejected, and all three Packers were ordered to fulfill their obligations.

The team played well throughout the appeals process, and was 7–2 by the time Hornung reported to Fort Riley, Kansas, on November 14, assigned to the 896th Engineer Floating Bridge Company, a National Guard unit. Nitschke and Dowler were valuable members of the team, but Hornung was a superstar—the preceding year, he had scored 176

ABOVE When the Packers recorded their first winning record in twelve seasons, Lombardi became a hero in Green Bay.

points, an NFL record that stood until 2006—and a favorite of Lombardi's. His plight became a national curiosity, as his absence robbed the Packers of their primary source of swagger. During the weeks of his Guard duty, the players would approach Lombardi asking, "Is Hornung going to make it?" They didn't ask about Nitschke or Dowler, who were equally important *on* the field.

Hornung missed a victory over the Rams, then managed to secure weekend passes for Green Bay's final four regular-season games, though he wasn't at his best. The Packers, however, looked stronger than ever. They finished 11-3 to capture the Western Conference, spurring local merchants to coin a moniker for Green Bay that may have seemed premature at the time, but later came to define the city's place at the center of the football universe—Titletown, USA.

Lombardi enlisted Kennedy himself to spring Hornung for the 1961 NFL Championship Game against the Giants. "I go back and pack and Kennedy calls Fort Riley and asks to speak to the camp commander, who is not there, so he finally

gets the company commander," Hornung recalled, according to Maraniss. "And he says, 'This is President Kennedy and I'm calling on behalf of Paul Hornung,' and the guy says, 'Yeah, and I'm Donald Duck.' But he got me out. A major came down and told me I could leave."

The title game proved to be the Packers' finest hour. Groundskeepers had dumped 20 tons of hay onto City Stadium, which a storm then covered with 14 inches of snow. But when everything was cleared, the field was in good shape, rendering conditions tolerable despite 20-degree weather.

The Packers broke open a scoreless tie with 24 second-quarter points and never looked back. Starr passed for three touchdowns, two to tight end Ron Kramer, and Hornung ran for 89 yards and scored a title-game record 19 points as Green Bay out-gained its rival 345 yards to 130.

Lombardi and his assistants moved their chess pieces masterfully that day. Giants coach Allie Sherman installed an odd, five-man line to surprise the Packers, but the home team adjusted its blocking schemes accordingly and had little trouble. When New York undershifted its line to take away Taylor's off-tackle slants—moving three of its linemen toward the weak side of the line and compensating by shifting its linebackers in the opposite direction—Green Bay ran right at ornery middle linebacker Sam Huff; right guard Forrest Gregg would simply block Huff in the direction he wanted to go, right tackle Norm Masters would attempt to seal the defensive end to the outside, and Taylor would hit the appropriate hole. On plays to the outside, Huff often found himself hammered by tight end Ron Kramer, who cracked back on him.

Kramer scored his touchdowns in flood-right formation. The Packers flooded the right side with three receivers to draw the coverage (especially Huff's). Kramer pretended to run block on the outside linebacker, then released into a pass route. On his first touchdown, a 14-yarder, he broke open in the vacated middle of the field and ran over a safety to score. On the second, he faked the same route over the middle, broke back outside and caught a 13-yard pass while tiptoeing along the sideline.

ABOVE Lombardi checks the field at City Stadium prior to the 1961 NFL title game. Workers used hay to keep the turf thawed.

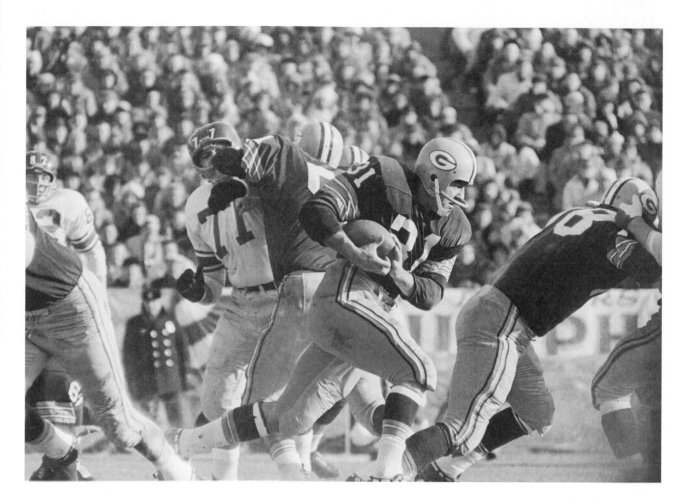

Lombardi rarely admitted to perfection, but after the game he told his players, "Today you were the best team in the history of the National Football League."

And they believed him. "We knew we were good. But then and there, we believed we were gonna be the best," guard Fuzzy Thurston says. "We had five years to stay together. And that game was the key."

The players left the field to standing ovations. A wild celebration rocked Green Bay that night, sparks literally flying downtown. Fans had tied one of the City Stadium goal posts to the bumper of a car, and were dragging it down the street.

The Packers picked up right where they left off in 1962. They won their first ten games and were rarely even challenged in doing so. They shut out three opponents during the run and held four others to fewer than ten points; their winning scores included 49–0 and 38–7 over the Bears, and 49–0 over the Eagles.

The only scar on the season was a 26–14 loss on Thanksgiving Day at Detroit, where the Lions' relentless defensive line terrorized Starr and sacked him eleven times. The inscrutable Lombardi could be furious after victories, sanguine after losses. "You didn't think we were going to win them all, did you?" he cheerfully asked Art Daley of the Green Bay *Press-Gazette* after the game.

According to his son in *The Essential Vince Lombardi*, this is what the coach said to his players after the loss: "Let it be an example to all of us. The Green Bay Packers are no better

ABOVE Fullback Jim Taylor chugs for yardage in the Packers' 37–0 rout of the Giants in 1961.

113

ABOVE Lombardi gets a victory ride after winning his first NFL championship.

than anyone else when they aren't ready, when they play as individuals and not as one. . . . Our greatest glory is not in never failing, but in rising every time we fall."

And rise they did. The team finished 13-1 in 1962 and traveled to New York for a championship rematch with the hated Giants.

Not all was right with Lombardi's squad. Hornung had a sore shoulder and knee, center Jim Ringo had a pinched nerve in his right arm, and Ron Kramer was generally battered. Taylor had lost 15 pounds in a few weeks; only later would doctors diagnose hepatitis.

Just as daunting was the weather in New York. It was 17 degrees at Yankee Stadium, with consistent gusts of wind up to 40 miles per hour. At one point, a group of Packers rose from their wooden bench to stand, and a gust blew the bench onto the field. Some of the players would swear it felt as cold as the immortal Ice Bowl played in Green Bay five years later. This was before the NFL took such good care of

the playing surface, and the turf was frozen solid in some places, rutted and pocked and sharp as shale in others. Tex Maule wrote in *Sports Illustrated* that it was "better suited to ice hockey than football."

But the Packers were equal to the challenge. Taylor was a workhorse, carrying the ball 31 times for 85 yards and constantly chiding the Giants to "hit me harder." The defense allowed just one touchdown, guard Jerry Kramer filled in for Hornung at placekicker and nailed three field goals, and Green Bay won again, 16–7. In a letter to his players after the victory, Lombardi wrote: "The Giants tried to intimidate us physically, but in the final analysis we were mentally tougher than they were, and that same mental toughness made them crack."

The Packers were kings, and the Lombardi mythos was about to explode. Already he was considered a miracle worker as a football coach. Soon he would be worshipped as a national icon, the symbol of what Americans aspired to.

ABOVE Swirling winds and sub-freezing temperatures made the 1962 NFL Championship Game a brutal contest.

THE OLD GUARD PREVAILS

THE SUPER BOWLS

11

After back-to-back NFL championships in 1961 and 1962,
it no doubt felt to Green Bay fans as though their team would never lose another meaningful game—the Packers looked all but invincible. NFL Commissioner Pete Rozelle sharply intruded on the reverie when, in April of '63, he suspended Paul Hornung indefinitely for betting on NFL games. The Packers had survived the halfback's induction into the National Guard in 1961, but his league-imposed banishment would prove more damaging.

Elijah Pitts and Tom Moore filled in at halfback, and guard Jerry Kramer took over placekicking duties. But Hornung simply had no replacement as a locker-room presence, or as an emotional buffer between Lombardi and his players. Injuries didn't help the matter. Bart Starr broke his hand that year, and middle linebacker Ray Nitschke broke his arm on Thanksgiving Day.

Green Bay finished 11-2-1, a half game behind the Chicago Bears in the Western Conference, and missed the championship game. The season also was marred by the assassination of President John F. Kennedy, who had formed a bond of mutual admiration with Lombardi.

Speaking to the local First Friday Club after the season, the coach sounded a challenge: "As far as the Packers are concerned, as someone once said, 'We are not slain, just

wounded. Let me lay awhile and bleed a little and I will rise to fight again.' So will the Packers. While this has been a very frustrating season, for many reasons, this team will always have a soft spot in my heart because of the many adversities and the many frustrations it had to meet."

Lombardi got Hornung back after a one-year absence in 1964, but the Golden Boy seemed to have lost his kicking touch. Missed field goals or extra points were pivotal in two Packers losses. And though Starr led the league in passing and the defense held opponents to a stingy 227 yards per game, the team finished 8-5-1, a record that chafed Lombardi.

The 1965 season began with changes. Marv Fleming and Dave Robinson were promoted to the starting lineup, Fleming at tight end and Robinson at outside linebacker. The

OPPOSITE Max McGee makes a juggling touchdown catch against the Chiefs in Super Bowl I at Los Angeles. **ABOVE** Lombardi's teams were at their best when it mattered most; his postseason record in Green Bay was 9-1.

117

ABOVE Lombardi and Don Chandler (top) after the kicker's field goal had beaten the Colts in overtime in a 1965 playoff. Jim Taylor (bottom) carries against the Browns in the 1965 NFL Championship Game.

coach brought in Don Chandler from the Giants to handle punting and kicking duties, and he acquired speedy flanker Carroll Dale from the Rams. By the start of the season, only eighteen of thirty-seven players remained from the 1962 championship team.

The new formula looked promising: the Packers began with a six-game winning streak, but ultimately fell into a tie with Baltimore at 10-3-1. That set up a classic playoff game. The Colts, without star quarterback Johnny Unitas and backup Gary Cuozzo, turned to Tom Matte, a halfback who taped the offensive plays to his wrist for reference. But Starr was knocked out of the game with bruised ribs on the first play from scrimmage, setting up a grueling defensive battle. Green Bay fell behind 10–0, but forced overtime with the help of Chandler's disputed 22-yard field goal. Colts fans still swear it was wide of the left upright; field judge Jim Tunney ruled it good. Chandler kicked another field goal in overtime to send the Packers to the championship game.

There, on a cold, muddy field in Green Bay, the Packers held superlative running back Jim Brown—who had sliced up the league for 1,544 yards in fourteen games during the regular season—to 50 yards and ground out a 23–12 victory. It was the Pack's third title under Lombardi, and its first in three years. Hornung and Jim Taylor had more success in the slop, combining for 201 rushing yards on forty-five carries.

"The snow and mud were our allies," Lombardi said after the game. "When you have conditions like these, it's best to be basic, not fancy. And we're the most basic offensive team there is."

Green Bay was restored to its place atop the NFL. That was nothing new. But the landscape of professional football was rapidly changing. The NFL had been engaged in a sometimes-bitter competition with the rival American Football League since 1960, and in '66 the two sides had agreed upon a historic merger. It would begin to take hold that season; teams from the two leagues would not play during the regular season, but they'd meet in January for a world championship that would soon be dubbed the Super Bowl.

The Super Bowl, of course, would become the preeminent sporting event in the nation, insinuating itself into American culture and obscuring the pro football that came before its birth. This can be a sore spot to some of the old Packers, who are proud of the earlier victory runs. "It irritates me now," says former wide receiver Boyd Dowler. "Like they didn't play championship games before 1966."

The looming AFL-NFL confrontation provided the backdrop for the '66 season, and the rivalry had a more direct impact on the Packers. A year earlier, Lombardi had drafted Texas Tech halfback Donny Anderson in the first round as a "future" pick. In 1966 he took Illinois fullback Jim Grabowski. To keep them out of AFL clutches, he paid them a total of $1 million—an exorbitant sum from a man infamous for his penny-pinching contract negotiations.

Taylor, who could be prickly, fumed over the rookies' salaries. After a game in October, he told the Associated Press that he planned to play out his option after the season. When it hit the newspapers, Lombardi was livid, first at Taylor and then at the wire service.

The drama didn't stop the Packers from winning, though. They lost only twice in 1966, by a combined total of four points, as the defense held six opponents to single-digit scoring.

The NFL championship that year went through Dallas. Tom Landry's team was emerging as Green Bay's biggest rival, and their New Year's game was a barnburner. The Packers kept staking leads, and the Cowboys kept fighting back to close the gap. Strong safety Tom Brown was nearly the goat of the game. He gave up a touchdown pass to tight end Frank Clarke, and was penalized for interfering with Clarke in the end zone with 1:52 left and the Packers up 34–27.

That put the ball on the Green Bay 2-yard line, but Phil Bengtson's defense rose up for one of its finest sequences and stopped the Cowboys on four straight plays. Brown redeemed himself by intercepting Don Meredith's pass with 28 seconds remaining.

"If God's got time to be a football fan, he musta really enjoyed this one," Meredith said.

Then came the Super Bowl and the AFL champions, the Kansas City Chiefs. Lombardi always got wound up for big games, but this one tied his stomach in knots. It wasn't that he was so worried about the Chiefs; the consensus among NFL stalwarts was that the AFL had many great players, but no great teams. But Lombardi felt the weight of representing an entire league. What if he let the game slip away? How could he live with the humiliation?

His angst was by no means lost on his players. "It was crystal clear," former guard Gale Gillingham says. "And then we didn't want to lose it either. We didn't want to lose for him, we didn't want to lose for the National Football League, and we didn't want to lose for ourselves."

"I think the pressure there could not be avoided," Dowler says. "We had everything to lose. We represented the establishment and the tradition of the NFL."

There was posturing before the game, mostly on the part of the Chiefs. They had a defensive back, Fred Williamson, who called himself the Hammer and described how he intended to knock out the Green Bay receivers. Mostly the Chiefs were miffed about being 13.5-point underdogs. "That is way out of line," fullback Curtis McClinton said. "The way I see it, they shouldn't be more than a three-point favorite. They get one point for the winning habit, one point because I think they are at the height of their maturity, and one point because they have a strong big-game history."

OPPOSITE Pregame introductions for the 1966 NFL title game in Dallas; that's tackle Forrest Gregg taking the field. **ABOVE** Bart Starr hands off to halfback Elijah Pitts in Super Bowl I.

121

The Packers were also thinking about the spread. "We have to show clearly just how big a difference there is between the two teams," Green Bay defensive end Lionel Aldridge said. "How bad should we beat them? I don't know, but one touchdown won't be enough."

On the bus ride to the game at the Los Angeles Coliseum, Lombardi sensed his team's unease, and he knew much of it trickled down from him. So did something completely spontaneous and a bit out of character: He asked the bus driver to pull over, stood in the aisle, and performed a soft shoe. To an extent, the troops' tension was cracked.

Still, the Packers played tentatively early on, and led only 14–10 at halftime. The Chiefs actually outgained the NFL team 181 yards to 164 in the first half. Lombardi had seen some encouraging signs, though. Tied 7–7 in the second quarter, Starr connected with Carroll Dale for a 64-yard touchdown pass that was called back because left tackle Bob Skoronski moved before the snap. Starr had suckered Williamson with a play-action fake on the third-and-1 play, and he felt he could use the tactic to exploit the Chiefs again.

In the second half, the Packers snapped out of their stupor. Safety Willie Wood got things rolling when he intercepted Len Dawson's pass on the first drive of the third quarter and ran to the Kansas City 5-yard line, setting up an off-tackle run by Elijah Pitts that made it 21–10. The Chiefs didn't threaten again, failing to cross Green Bay's 40-yard line in the second half, and the Packers won 35–10.

"The way I see it, we lost our poise after Wood's interception," Kansas City defensive end Jerry Mays told *Sports Illustrated* after the game. "The Packers themselves beat us in the first half, then the Packers and the Packer myth beat us in the second."

The surprise hero for Green Bay was veteran receiver Max McGee. He had caught only four passes during the regular season, so he saw no harm in partying most of the night before the Super Bowl. But Dowler re-injured his shoulder blocking on the game's first series, and McGee went the rest of the game, catching seven passes for 138 yards and a pair of touchdowns.

Both teams were conciliatory afterward, and the Chiefs seemed suitably impressed by Green Bay's execution. "They don't hit harder than anyone else," linebacker Sherrill Headrick said. "The thing is, they never block the wrong man—they're always in your way. And their backs always hit the hole. On their sweeps I was getting blocked by a different guy each time—the tight end, the pulling guard, the back. I don't know where they all came from."

The Packers were imbued with a mixture of relief and joy as they headed into 1967. They wanted to become the first NFL team since the Packers of 1929-31 to win three consecutive titles, and the first to do it decisively, with official championship games. It wouldn't come without adjustments, though. Taylor bolted for the expansion New Orleans Saints, and Hornung soon followed. Lombardi did not protect the oft-injured halfback in the Saints' veteran-allocation draft, and they snatched him up. The loss of his favorite athlete nearly crushed Lombardi.

The Packers lost their final two games of the 1967 regular season, but managed to capture the newly constructed Central Division with a 9-4-1 record. In the Western Conference championship, they faced the Rams, who had beaten them 27–24 in Los Angeles just two weeks earlier. "I remember giving the team a slogan for that week and it was, 'Run to win.' I took it from St. Paul in the Bible. To beat the Rams we had to run on them and we had to beat their strength, which was Deacon Jones and Merlin Olsen, and that offensive line of ours did the job," the coach explained in *Lombardi on Football*.

The Packers prevailed, 28–7, then survived the famed Ice Bowl a week later. Super Bowl II was against the Oakland Raiders and their brash young general manager, Al Davis.

It was a tired group that traveled from Green Bay to balmy Miami. The team had been through a lot, including a plague of injuries. Lombardi whipped up some energy the

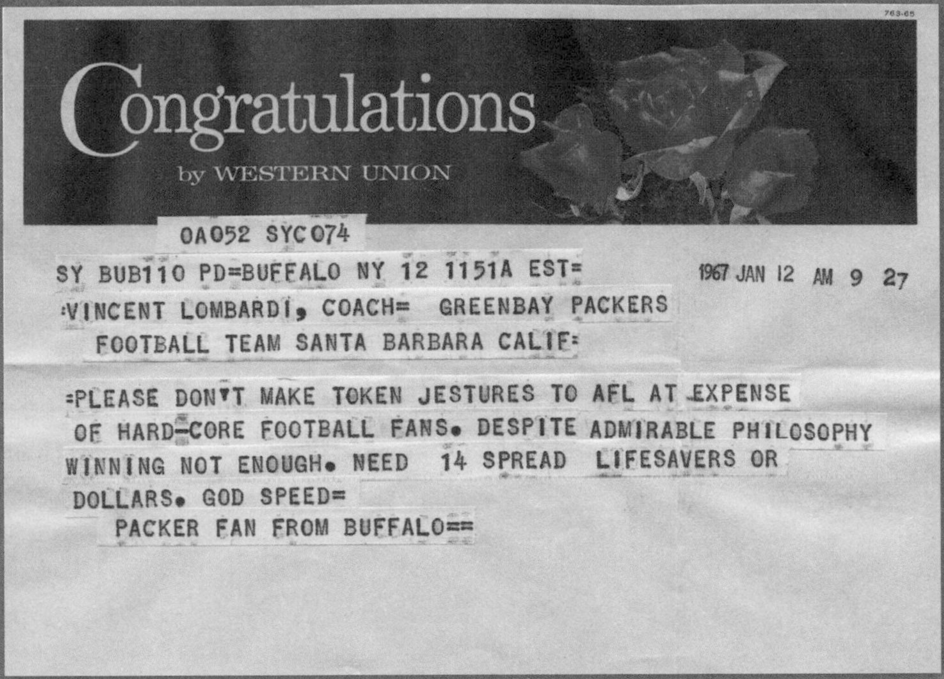

Congratulations
by WESTERN UNION

763-65

0A052 SYC074

SY BUB110 PD=BUFFALO NY 12 1151A EST=   1967 JAN 12 AM 9 27

:VINCENT LOMBARDI, COACH= GREENBAY PACKERS
    FOOTBALL TEAM SANTA BARBARA CALIF=

:PLEASE DON'T MAKE TOKEN JESTURES TO AFL AT EXPENSE
OF HARD-CORE FOOTBALL FANS. DESPITE ADMIRABLE PHILOSOPHY
WINNING NOT ENOUGH. NEED 14 SPREAD LIFESAVERS OR
DOLLARS. GOD SPEED=
    PACKER FAN FROM BUFFALO==

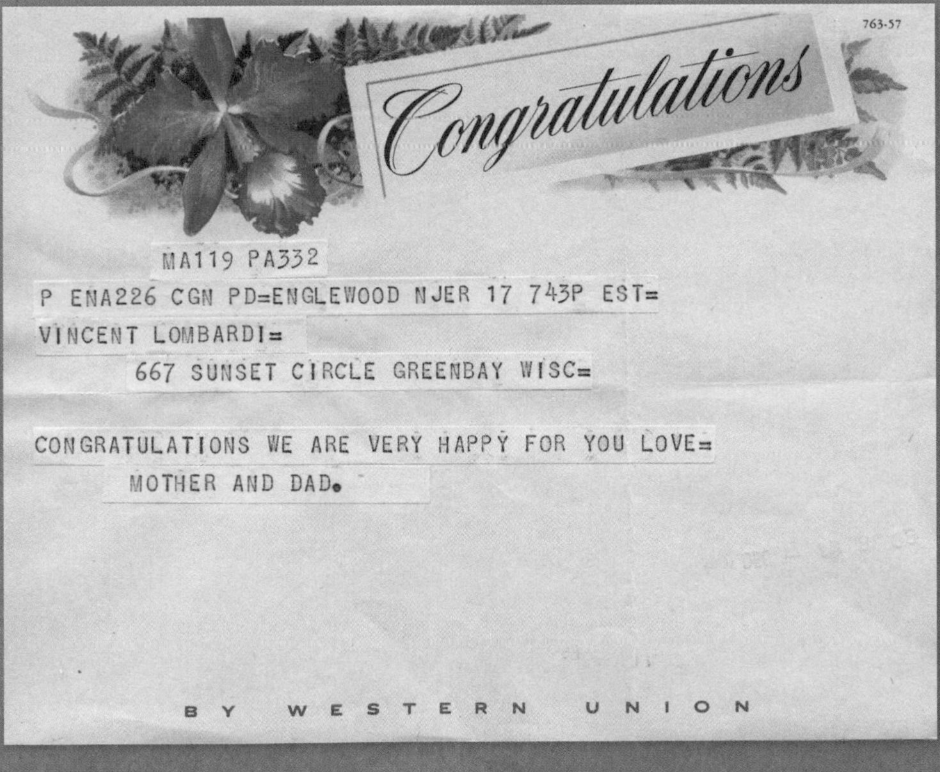

763-57

Congratulations

MA119 PA332

P ENA226 CGN PD=ENGLEWOOD NJER 17 743P EST=

VINCENT LOMBARDI=

    667 SUNSET CIRCLE GREENBAY WISC=

CONGRATULATIONS WE ARE VERY HAPPY FOR YOU LOVE=
    MOTHER AND DAD.

BY WESTERN UNION

ABOVE Super Bowl I brought a flood of telegrams, the senders including a displaced Packers fan and Lombardi's parents.

21 NA **76** **99**
ENTER GATE   SECTION   ROW   SEAT

WORLD CHAMPIONSHIP GAME
AFL VS NFL-SUNDAY, JAN.14,1968

ORANGE BOWL, MIAMI, FLA.
3:00 PM   EST. PRICE $11.64   **$12.00**
            STATE TAX $ .36
This ticket cannot be refunded

AFL-NFL WORLD CHAMPIONSHIP GAME
ORANGE BOWL, MIAMI, FLA. $12.00
SUNDAY, JANUARY 14, 1968·3:00 PM

week before the Bowl, reminding his players that Oakland had given a pretty good 49ers team a stern test in a 1967 preseason game.

Lombardi was dropping hints of his retirement, an event that had been rumored for more than a year, and the atmosphere became charged as the game approached. Guard Jerry Kramer, who was working on a book project, sneaked a tape recorder into the locker room before Super Bowl II, and now offers audio through his website. Kramer captured Skoronski delivering an emotional pregame speech.

"We've dedicated a lot of games over the years to coaches, people," Skoronski said, the big man's voice quavering. "And today, fellas, there's a lot of guys who have built the Packers into what they are today who might be playing their last game. I'm asking every guy here to go out and play his goddamn level best for these guys who have had a lot to do with the Green Bay Packers. Boys, we're wounded, but we're not dead."

No, they weren't. The Raiders were never really in this game.

Oakland used an odd defensive front, with a man directly over the center, the defensive tackles even with the offensive tackles, and a linebacker in front of each guard. This made the Raiders hard to attack in the middle, so Lombardi and Starr turned to sweeps, off-tackle runs, and quick flare passes to the halfback. McGee had a big 35-yard gain on classic third-and-1 play-action, and Starr beat a blitz to find Dowler for a 62-yard touchdown. Green Bay ran for 160 yards, Starr passed for 202, and the Packers romped 33–14. As the seconds ticked away, Jerry Kramer and Forrest Gregg hoisted Lombardi onto their shoulders and carried him from the field one last time. "It was to win three straight, something we'd always wanted to do," Dowler says. "It would have been anti-climactic to lose."

The Packers had their climax. Soon enough, the Lombardi era would be over. The coach was about to pitch both himself and his team into unfamiliar waters.

ABOVE Back when the Super Bowl was officially called the AFL-NFL World Championship Game, and a $12 ticket price couldn't ensure a sellout. **OPPOSITE** Gregg and Kramer give the coach a victory ride after Super Bowl II, Lombardi's last game in Green Bay.

12

COLD COMFORT
THE ICE BOWL

Basketball and hockey are played in climate-controlled arenas. Baseball games are canceled when it rains. Ditto track meets, tennis matches, and stock car races. Even many NFL games are now played under domes, where players, coaches, and fans alike can pretend the elements don't exist.

For much of the league's history, though, football games have been played in whatever nature had to offer—snow, sleet, rain, mud, wind, or late-summer humidity. Sometimes the results are frustrating, other times almost comical. On occasion, however, the result is nothing short of brutal.

Never has this been truer than on New Year's Eve, 1967, when the Packers hosted the Dallas Cowboys in the NFL Championship Game. The image of that game still sends shivers down the spine of anyone who witnessed it live. Almost immediately it became known as the Ice Bowl. "Being honest, I always thought freezing was freezing until I went to Green Bay," says former Cowboys halfback Dan Reeves, who went on to a long NFL coaching career.

Part of the lore of the Ice Bowl—in 2000, visitors to nfl. com voted it the most memorable game in history—is how off-guard it caught everybody. Nobody was worried about the field. Lombardi had ordered the installation of an $80,000 heat-exchange system under the turf, a series of 750,000-volt coils buried six inches below the surface and designed to

keep the grass thawed. Anyway, December 30 in Green Bay was relatively mild, with a high of 19 degrees.

The visiting Cowboys had good practices in the days leading up to the contest. On game day, Sunday morning, Reeves and fullback Walt Garrison headed for their pregame meal in coats and ties. "We got out there and said, 'Whoa, we'd better get our overcoats,'" Reeves recalls. "We had maybe forty yards between the hotel and the restaurant, and we were sprinting. We got in there and said, 'Man, it's cold!' And the waitress said, 'Well, it should be. It's thirteen below.' We laughed. We thought she was kidding. It had dropped thirty-two degrees overnight."

It had, with little warning, become the coldest New Year's Eve in Green Bay history, with a wind-chill factor of minus 48 degrees.

It *never* dropped 32 degrees overnight in Dallas. Truth be told, though, even the Wisconsin natives weren't ready

---

OPPOSITE Green Bay fans settle in for a brutal day of football at Lambeau Field on December 31, 1967. **ABOVE** A bundled Lombardi watches from the sidelines. Behind him is backup quarterback Zeke Bratkowski.

for this sort of chill. NFL Commissioner Pete was in attendance, and many players expected him to postpone the game. They looked at each other nervously in the locker rooms, and Rozelle never issued a proclamation. The game would go on.

Lombardi's acclaimed heating coils had failed in the Arctic blast, and the turf at Lambeau Field was a solid sheet of ice. The referees' whistles didn't work; the little wooden balls inside the whistles had frozen. Players found it difficult to catch or kick the ball, and nearly impossible to cut sharply. "I held for field goals and extra points," Reeves says. "We went out for pregame warm-ups, and we only kicked five or six balls. We hardly couldn't catch it. I never felt anything close to that in a game."

In the stands, fans packed themselves into layers of protective clothing—down sleeping bags over full-body hunting suits over parkas over flannel shirts over underclothes over longjohns. They stacked cardboard under

their feet so their shoes wouldn't have to touch the ground, and they drank near-toxic levels of whiskey and brandy. They exhaled so much steam just watching the game that it was sometimes hard for fans in upper rows to see the field clearly. Four had heart attacks in the stands, and one elderly spectator died.

Everyone was affected, including the TV announcers. Frank Gifford, Lombardi's former halfback in New York, was calling the game for CBS. "I think I'll take another bite of my coffee," Gifford grumbled on-air.

Some of the Packers wanted to wear gloves, but Lombardi said only linemen could protect their hands that way. Linebacker Dave Robinson wore brown gloves anyway, figuring (correctly) that they matched his complexion fairly well and the coach wouldn't notice. Some players had a harder time than others. Bob Hayes, the Dallas wide receiver who had been an Olympic sprinter, had grown up in Jacksonville, Florida, and was absolutely miserable. Green Bay cornerback Herb

ABOVE Fashion took a back seat to survival as the wind-chill factor hit minus 48 degrees at Lambeau.

ABOVE Lombardi had to adapt his game plan to conditions that made throwing, kicking, and cutting impractical.

Adderley figured out that if Hayes put his hands down his pants at the line, it was a run play. Hands out, it was a pass. "Whenever Herb saw that, he cheated over to the middle," former Packers guard Jerry Kramer says. "He picked off a pass because of that."

Other players found ways to cope. "At some point you had to deal with it or give up," Kramer says. "It was like, 'OK, I'm freezing my butt off. But we're gonna play, so let's play. We'll be cold tomorrow.'"

"The coaches had a great deal to do with that," says Bart Starr, the Packers' quarterback that day. "Coach Lombardi was one tough hombre. He had a way of conveying toughness."

The Dallas coach, Tom Landry, was much less emotional, less bombastic than Lombardi. But in his silent way, the Texan was just as tough. Landry had been the chief defensive assistant in New York when Lombardi was the Giants' top offensive assistant, and the two shared a simmering if respectful rivalry.

It's interesting to note that the Cowboys and Packers played for the NFL title twice in one calendar year. Three-hundred and sixty-four days before the Ice Bowl, on January 1, 1967, they had squared off in Dallas for the 1966 championship. Though less hallowed than the Ice Bowl, that game was even more entertaining. It took a goal-line stand in the final two minutes to preserve Green Bay's 34–27 victory, Tom Brown intercepting Don Meredith's pass in the end zone with 28 seconds left.

Nearly a year later, the teams couldn't muster such a scoring output. They did stage something that looked like a football game, though.

Just as they had done in the 1966 title game, the Packers jumped to a 14–0 lead, this time on two touchdown passes from Starr to Boyd Dowler. But Dallas turned the tide in the second quarter. Cowboys defensive end George Andrie picked up Starr's fumble and lurched seven yards for a touchdown, and Danny Villanueva soon followed that up with a short field goal after Willie Wood had fumbled a punt. It was 14–10 Green Bay at halftime.

Exhaustion and discomfort began to show in the second half as the weather took its toll. Neither team scored in the third quarter. "I remember not feeling anything," Reeves says. "I remember getting my lip busted, and no blood came out. We had a possession in the third quarter, a six- or seven-minute drive. I was breathing hard, and my throat burned from breathing in that cold air."

Meredith, the Dallas quarterback, came down with pneumonia after the game and was hospitalized upon his return to Texas. Several players developed frostbite, including Starr. His recurs every once in a while on the tips of his fingers. Referee Norm Schachter's foot was frostbitten, too, in the left heel. "It showed up as blisters, like you had touched a hot stove," Kramer says.

"Surprisingly, the guys who were able to wear gloves had it worst," Reeves says. "Back then players wore cotton gloves. They think what happened is that they'd stand in front of those air blowers, warming their hands. Their hands would perspire, then freeze."

Early in the fourth quarter, the Cowboys did something few NFL teams could pull off—they caught the Packers by surprise. Reeves took a handoff, started to his left, then stopped and lofted a pass downfield to flanker Lance Rentzel. It was a halfback option, right out of Lombardi's playbook. "I kept my hand in my pants until the last second (before the snap), so at least I could feel the ball," Reeves says.

His pass to Rentzel was on target, and the Cowboys had themselves a 50-yard touchdown play and a 17–14 lead that stunned the already-numb home crowd.

Green Bay got the ball on its 32-yard line with 4:50 remaining in the game. Starr had by now led his team on many fourth-quarter comebacks, but the conditions of the Ice Bowl demanded a unique effort. "This is it," the quarterback told his teammates in the huddle. "We're going in."

Starr soon had the Packers in Dallas territory, and his 19-yard connection with fullback Chuck Mercein on a swing pass to the left took them to the 11-yard line. Mercein, born in Milwaukee and educated at Yale, was a midseason pickup for

Lombardi, a castoff from the Giants. But he was a major player in the Ice Bowl. After Mercein's 19-yard reception, Starr went to him again, on what the Hall of Fame quarterback proudly remembers as the greatest single play call of his career.

All day long the Packers had been trying to sweep to the right, and Dallas defensive tackle Bob Lilly had been disrupting the play. He was an incredibly quick 260-pounder who shot into gaps before being blocked and chased down sweeps from behind. Starr waited until the crucial point in the game to call Give 54. It was a sucker play, or influence play, designed to take advantage of Lilly's ferocity. It looked like a sweep, with the guards pulling right. Starr opened up as if to hand to the halfback, but instead gave the ball to Mercein, who ran cleanly through the hole vacated by the pursuing Lilly. "Our guard, Gale Gillingham, pulled, and Bob Lilly followed him," Starr says. "The crucial block was by (tackle) Bob Skoronski (on the defensive end). He deserves a tremendous amount of credit. If the footing was better, Chuck may have scored."

As it was, Mercein bulled for eight yards, down to the Dallas 3-yard line. Halfback Donnie Anderson then picked up the first down at the 1, but he found no traction on two subsequent handoffs and barely got back to the line of scrimmage.

It was third-and-goal, 16 seconds left.

The Packers knew from film study that Dallas defensive tackle Jethro Pugh tended to rise up out of his stance early. Starr wondered if his line could execute a wedge play, where the blockers squeeze in close, practically arm to arm, and simply push forward as a massive bubble. He asked Kramer and center Ken Bowman if they could wedge Pugh. They thought they could, and Starr called his final timeout to confer with Lombardi.

The safe call would have been a pass. It wasn't that throwing the ball, or catching it, would have been easy this New Year's Eve. But if the pass should fall incomplete, the Packers could tie the game with a short field goal on

fourth down and head into overtime, as painful as that may have sounded. Starr suggested Brown Right 31 Wedge. Except instead of giving the ball to the fullback as the play required, Starr would keep it himself—unbeknownst to any of his teammates.

"Run it," Lombardi replied, "and let's get the hell out of here."

Kramer then got the best news of the day as he lined up for the make-or-break play. "I found a divot," he says. "It was small, but it felt like a starting block. My left foot just fit snugly. I got a wonderful start. When Jethro got up in the air and started backwards, I knew the game was over."

Kramer and Bowman shot forward on a quick count. They blocked for the wedge, and Starr dove into the frozen end zone. Mercein didn't realize Starr had kept the ball until he saw the No. 15 on the QB's back, and he wound up landing on top of him. The moment is immortalized in a photograph by

John Biever, who was fifteen years old at the time. His father, Vernon Biever, was the Packers' team photographer, and had stationed his son behind the end zone while the older man prowled the Green Bay sidelines looking for reaction shots from Lombardi.

In the 1966 NFL title game, the Cowboys had been unable to punch it in for the winning score as time expired. A year later, the Packers showed them how to do it. Green Bay had won again, delaying Dallas' ascendancy and earning the right to play in their second Super Bowl. Afterward, Cowboys coach Tom Landry still couldn't believe Lombardi had ordered a running play. "It was a dumb call," he remarked. "Now it's a great play."

But Lombardi didn't see it that way. "If you can't run the ball in there in a moment of crisis, you don't deserve to win," he noted. "These decisions don't come from the mind, they come from the gut."

ABOVE The game might have been even harder on warm-weather Cowboys like Dick Daniels (21) and Bob Hayes (22).

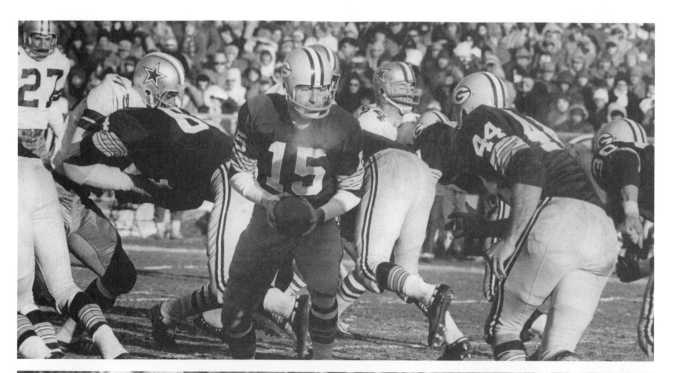

ABOVE Bart Starr hands off to Donny Anderson (44, top). Starr's 1-yard dive on the final play (bottom) iced the game.

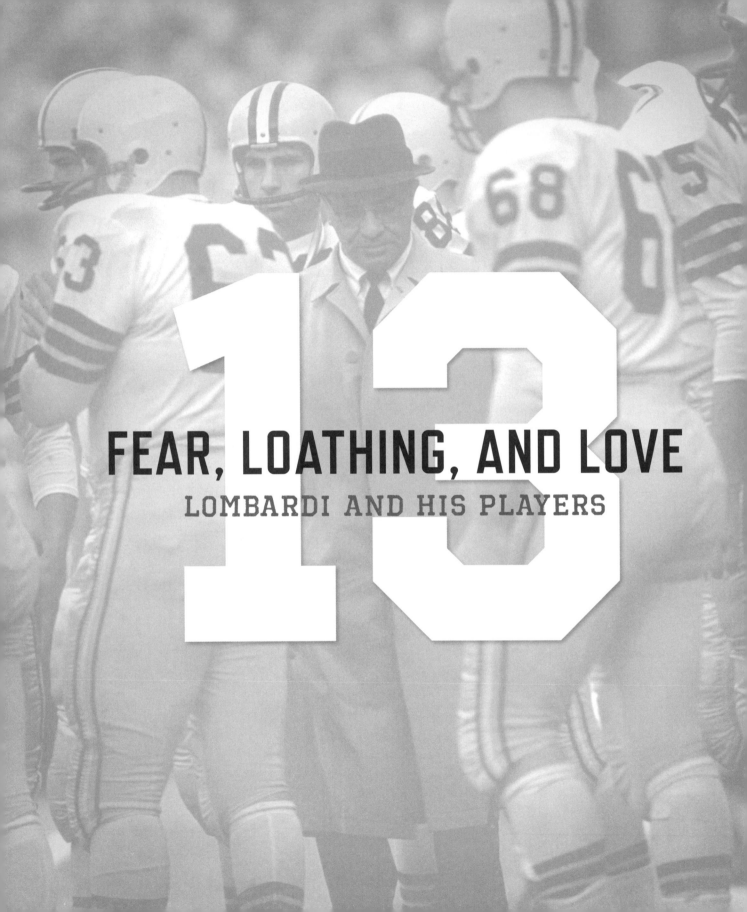

FEAR, LOATHING, AND LOVE
LOMBARDI AND HIS PLAYERS

13

Some people dream that they show up for a college class and realize there's a final exam they had forgotten to study for. Others dream of missing flights or walking into the office in their underwear. Paul Hornung's nightmare involved Vince Lombardi.

"I had a dream the other night that I came by and sneaked Max McGee out after hours," he told *Sports Illustrated* the week before Super Bowl II. "Vinnie found out about it and darned if he didn't fine me five-thousand bucks, even if I wasn't with the team any longer. The thing that woke me up was that I dreamed I paid the fine."

Keep in mind that Hornung was arguably Lombardi's favorite player. And that he had spent his last days in the NFL in 1967 in training camp with the New Orleans Saints, far from the coach's sphere of influence.

A man of baritone voice, seething emotions and indomitable will, Lombardi had the capacity to frighten that most leaders would envy. Everyone in the organization, from club directors to assistant coaches to secretaries, shrank from the coach's sourer moods. "It became a reciprocal thing: Don't tell on me and I won't tell on you," one former assistant told David Maraniss, author of *When Pride Still Mattered*. "Sooner or later you knew you were going to screw up in a way he wouldn't like if he found out. That bonded everyone together."

Intimidated? "Completely," former guard Fuzzy Thurston admits. "You were scared to death you would ever make a mistake."

Little wonder. Just get a look at sideline videos of Lombardi coaching the Packers. One, a 1968 NFL Films released simply titled *Lombardi*, shows the coach at his most irascible. At one point he yells to his defense, "Everybody grabbing out there, nobody tackling! Just grabbing, everybody. Grab, grab, grab. Put your shoulder in it!"

In another shot, as some of his players leave the field in a game against the Rams, Lombardi says to one of them: "What the hell is wrong with you, anyway?"

OPPOSITE Lombardi in 1959: His gruff personality and demanding regimen were a shock to the Packers. **ABOVE** The coach didn't actually do a lot of coaching on the sideline, which freed him up for pointed comments on his players' efforts.

135

And those were semi-public moments. Imagine the coach on the practice field, or worse yet, behind closed doors. Jesse Whittenton, a former Green Bay defensive back, remembers the arrival of Louis Hernandez, a guard from UTEP who was drafted in 1963. The Packers' brain trust thought Hernandez was a great prospect. But he showed up to training camp at well over 300 pounds, and Lombardi was incensed. He rode the rookie without mercy, physically and mentally. During one scrimmage, Lombardi pulled the young giant aside and yelled, "Hernandez, you're not only fat, but you're stupid!"

"We all kind of snickered," Whittenton recalls. "And he turned around and jumped all over Bart [Starr] and said something like, 'What are you laughing at? You're throwing too many interceptions.' Bart was just in the wrong place."

Another wrong place to be was the training room. During his first camp in De Pere, Lombardi was disgusted to find a large contingent of Packers getting treatment for ailments real and imagined. He angrily shooed them away. Lombardi once ordered Ron Kramer back onto the practice field after the tight end had turned an ankle, and Kramer never again removed himself without permission.

If only Lombardi had held himself to the same standards. He was often hurt while playing at Fordham, and was reportedly something of a hypochondriac when it came to his own aches and pains.

ABOVE Lombardi instructs his players—including linebacker Ray Nitschke—at practice.

Lombardi had rules for public behavior and attendance, and he meted out fines liberally. In 1959, his first season in Green Bay, Whittenton, Hornung, McGee and fullback Howie Ferguson checked in early, then went out on the town. The next day, Lombardi introduced himself and immediately levied fines.

"Fined? What for?" the players asked.

"You missed curfew," Lombardi explained.

"Curfew? It doesn't start until tonight," they pleaded.

"Mister, curfew started the day you brought your bags into camp," was the coach's retort.

"Right then we knew what we were in for," Whittenton says, shaking his head.

So what if Lombardi dumped the fine money into a fund for postseason parties, and once forgave McGee his debts when he signed a new contract? He had still managed to establish an effective deterrent.

The penalties in Green Bay went beyond the monetary. Lombardi wasn't above publicly humiliating his players. He'd stop practice to chew them out, or re-run the film projector several times to highlight their mistakes in Tuesday film sessions. "We watched film together as an offense, and nobody said anything but him," former receiver Boyd Dowler says. "Sometimes it was loud, and not so pleasant."

"The only thing I hated was Tuesday morning," Thurston says. "He'd ream our ass."

Lombardi and his assistants would grade their players on every snap, and those grades would be posted for all to see on Thursdays. "He gave us a twenty-dollar bill if we made our blocking percentage," Kramer says. "I think in three years I only missed one. That's why he and I got along pretty good. I had my own personality: I'm here, let's get on with it. No B.S." For anyone who *hadn't* made his blocks, Thursdays were to be dreaded.

Sometimes Lombardi's punishment was more creative. One time Whittenton, Thurston, halfback Lew Carpenter, and defensive end Bill Quinlan sneaked out after curfew and headed for a bar. Lombardi found out. After practice

the next day, he kept the rest of the team on the field and ordered the four criminals to leapfrog around the perimeter of the field like second graders. "And my arm was in a cast," Whittenton says. "Those big fat linemen, I couldn't hardly get over them. That was tough. It wasn't the work. It was the embarrassment."

Yet Whittenton doesn't seem to begrudge the mockery. "I think the fine was only $150," he says. "We knew we did wrong, we got caught. We got off pretty easy, really."

If malingering was a misdemeanor and skipping curfew a felony in Lombardi's legal code, mental mistakes on the field were practically capital offenses. And it didn't matter if they came in a preseason game, or even a one-sided victory. "He wasn't that tough if you missed a block,"

ABOVE Injuries had to be serious in Green Bay, where the coach had little patience for perceived malingering.

137

Thurston says. "But if you missed a mental assignment during a game, oh, boy."

Lombardi knew how overbearing he could be. He just couldn't stop himself. "Hell, I can't just sit around and see an error being made and not say anything about it," Vince Jr. quotes him as saying in *The Essential Vince Lombardi*. "I like to think I've had some experience in this business, and you don't win when you're making lots of errors. Nobody wants to be told he's making errors, not the way I tell them. But they've got to be told and told until they get to the point where they don't make them anymore."

Not everybody responded to Lombardi's style with awe or amusement. He rubbed some players the wrong way, and they usually didn't last long in Green Bay. Asked by NFL Films about the effect of his hectoring on players, Lombardi said, "I'm not worried about their morale. I'm worried about Vince Lombardi's morale."

Defensive end Jim Temp played two years under Lombardi, until a shoulder injury derailed his career, and he is clearly conflicted by his memories of the Hall of Fame coach. "Some players with potential, he wrecked them," Temp says. "Others, he made them great."

Each year the University of Wisconsin coaching staff would trek from Madison to De Pere to work the Packers' training camp for a day. One year, Temp recalls, the roster included a young guard who had played at Wisconsin. "[Lombardi] blistered him five, six, seven times in practice, in front of his college coaches," Temp says. "Behind it all, there was a psychology—'I'll be so good you won't be able to say a damn thing.' I thought, 'You SOB, what's the matter with you?'"

ABOVE Lombardi leads the Packers in prayer, or at least in a sideline pep talk. **OPPOSITE** The coach with four of his offensive leaders: center Jim Ringo (51), receiver Boyd Dowler (86), tight end Ron Kramer (88), and quarterback Bart Starr (15).

ABOVE Contrary to his public image, the old man could enjoy lighter moments on the field.

Temp is a thoughtful man who served for years on the Packers' executive committee. But he is clearly in the minority opinion on this subject. Most of Lombardi's players were abused and humiliated—and came away with nothing but respect for the boss.

"Lombardi was the kind of guy who could talk to you in such a way that he'd cut your guts out, and five minutes later you love him all over again," Hall of Fame defensive end Willie Davis observes. "Because you knew anything harsh he was saying to you was about making you a better football player."

Ron Kramer has heard Lombardi portrayed as a foul-mouthed dictator and a bully. "Who says that? I'll tell you who," Kramer says angrily. "It's those wackos writing books and those wackos writing newspaper articles. He was the greatest, most personable guy you've ever seen. He'd play in our gin tournaments and cribbage tournaments. He'd throw his ten bucks in. He was our kind of guy, man. I wouldn't have wanted him any different. People say Vince Lombardi was tough. I say you should have met my old man."

Dowler tends to speak in more level tones, but notes that Lombardi was equally quick to praise or to criticize, depending on your performance, and wasn't all business. "Practice was very intense, though it could be a lot of fun," he says. "He could relax, he could laugh. He certainly wasn't the big ogre some in the media turned him into. He could get under your skin. He knew your hot spots."

"Nobody likes to get screamed at," former guard Gale Gillingham says. "But if you were gonna be there, that was the only way. It was his way or the highway. It didn't bother me as much as some probably. We got hollered at at home, too."

As Kramer suggests, Lombardi's players—at least those who stuck around a long time or made it into his inner circle—also saw his more human face. His laugh could be as infectious as his anxiety. True, he might spend ten minutes barking at a player if he blocked an opponent with the wrong shoulder. He also wasn't afraid to give the Packers a

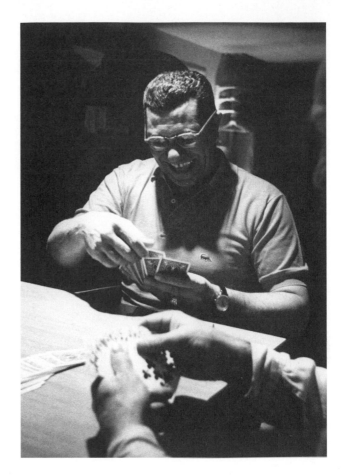

long speech on the meaning of love. In fact, Lombardi often referred to his Packers as a family, presumably seeing himself as the authoritarian but loving dad.

In the 1960s, playing the father figure on an NFL team meant going to bat for black players. Lombardi was sure he had failed to win jobs in the coaching ranks because of his Italian heritage, and he wouldn't stand for bigotry. After being forced to house his white and black players in separate accommodations for a 1960 preseason game in the South, Lombardi vowed never to let that happen again. Tavern and restaurant owners in the Green Bay area knew that if they excluded African-Americans, none of the Packers would be allowed to patronize them.

"If I ever hear 'nigger' or 'dago' or 'kike' or anything like that around here, regardless of who you are, you're

ABOVE Lombardi would often "throw his ten bucks in" and play in the Packers' gin and cribbage tournaments.

141

through with me," he once told his team, according to Vince Lombardi Jr. "You can't play for me if you have any kind of prejudice."

That was the high-minded way to characterize Lombardi's handling of his players. Henry Jordan put it another way: "He treats us all the same—like dogs."

Really, Lombardi did not treat all of the Packers the same. He seemed to know which buttons to push, and when, to get the most from each player. He knew which of them had to be lashed, and which needed a little coddling. "Henry Jordan has a tendency to be satisfied, which is why I don't flatter him much, and why often, when we're reviewing the pictures, I make him a target," Lombardi once said. "Sometimes you will make a man a target to impress somebody else who can't accept public criticism, but I will call Hank because we both know his ability and know that I'm on him to bring it out, and because he performs best when he's just a little upset."

Lombardi's mood swings were legendary, but they may have been more orchestrated than he let on. His son, Vince Jr., wrote that several times during his childhood, he walked into his father's office or the Green Bay locker room and found him trying on different facial expressions in front of a mirror.

"The secret of Vince Lombardi's success is that he used every type of persuasion known—charm, anger, laughter, tears, nagging, pleading, coaxing, demanding—to make every single person in his organization do the best job he was humanly capable of performing," defensive assistant Phil Bengtson once said, as repeated in Bob Rubin's *Return to Glory*.

His timing was mysterious to outsiders. After two fumbles and a blocked punt contributed to a 23–10 Thanksgiving Day loss at Detroit that dropped the Packers to 5–4 in 1960, his players expected the worst. But as Maraniss points out, Lombardi let them drink two beers on the flight home, gave them an energetic pep talk and later that night brought them and their families downtown for a turkey dinner at the Elks Club.

Yet he could be blistering after an easy victory. "I'd been in college and five years with the Rams, and everywhere I'd been, the deal was if you won the game, it was all celebration," notes former flanker Carroll Dale. "In Green Bay, if we won, you might go into the locker room and think it was the losers' room. Because he understood that people are more receptive to correction when you win. If you'd lose, there'd still be corrections but they'd be mild. If you won, he'd berate you. I still maintain today that was one of his great attributes."

Dale also credits Lombardi for declining to "jerk people around." He says he never worried that he'd be pulled from a game for making a mistake, or lose his starting job after one bad performance, and that it made him a more focused player. But Lombardi occasionally used this tool as well. In 1965, he benched his famous but struggling halfback, Hornung, for an entire game. The next week, the recommitted Hornung was back in the lineup, and he scored five touchdowns against the Colts.

Yes, Lombardi may have been great with the Xs and Os, and an astute judge of talent, and great with an organizational flow chart. But his skills of psychoanalysis may have been just as important. "If we missed a block, we paid for it," says Forrest Gregg, who became arguably the greatest offensive tackle in NFL history under Lombardi's guidance. "But I felt that was one way he had of motivating us to be better. And it also built confidence in us that he did expect us never to get beat. You might think sometimes, 'I don't know whether I can beat this guy.' But he'd expect it, so you'd say, 'Well, he thinks I can, so maybe I can.' "

That was one reason Lombardi's players put up with his outbursts and criticisms over most of a decade and never mutinied. Another was the era; Lombardi's brand of tough love might not find such a receptive audience today. And there was an additional reason the Packers bought into his approach: It helped them win five NFL championships.

"We had fun, we enjoyed what we did," former tight end Ron Kramer says. "But the greatest fun we had with Vince Lombardi was winning."

OPPOSITE Jim Taylor and Paul Hornung (5) bear Lombardi from the field after the 1965 NFL title game.

14

GONE, BUT NOT FORGOTTEN

LOMBARDI'S LEGACY

The Green Bay Packers' board of directors may very well have been happy to keep Vince Lombardi on the sidelines forever, or at least until he was 100. They had, in fact, extended his contract three times over the years, the last one an eight-year extension in November 1965. And why not? Lombardi had restored the NFL's smallest market to its place of honor, and had turned the Packers into the envy of the sports world.

Lombardi, though, was increasingly burdened by his job. No one talked about "burnout" in those days, as they did when John Madden retired after the 1978 season, or Bill Walsh walked away after 1988. But the coach seemed spent by his perpetual search for perfection.

As detailed by David Maraniss in *When Pride Still Mattered*, Lombardi's health had been in gradual decline, and seemed to worsen more rapidly in 1967. He was often seen with a bottle of antacid in his hand, and the arthritis in his left hip was starting to hobble him. Lombardi took indomethacin for the arthritis, and it caused an ulcer, adding to his misery.

Chuck Lane, one of the Packers' publicity men, told Maraniss that the coach twice blacked out in the team dressing room, and several times complained of shortness of breath or chest pain. Friends said he looked worn, and they were sure

the job was doing it to him. During his final run of championships, Lombardi confided to his assistants at training camp that he had dreamed of standing on a mountaintop and struggling to keep his footing while people tried to push him over the side.

"You know, the pressure of losing is bad, awful, because it kills you eventually," Lombardi would tell *Sports Illustrated* in 1969. "But the pressure of winning is worse, infinitely worse, because it keeps on torturing you and torturing you and torturing you. At Green Bay, I was winning one championship after another, after another, after another. I couldn't take it, because I blamed myself, damned myself whenever they lost a game."

So Lombardi ended the torture and announced his resignation shortly after Super Bowl II. He would continue as the Packers' general manager, would still keep an office at team headquarters, lending his considerable reputation and his expertise in personnel evaluation. But no longer would he walk the sidelines in his camel hair coat.

OPPOSITE Lombardi had a genius for leadership, but the pressure of winning eventually wore him down. **ABOVE** The coach at Wrigley Field in Chicago.

Green Bay Packers

1265 LOMBARDI AVENUE / GREEN BAY, WISCONSIN 54303 ; AREA CODE 414 494-2351

February 4, 1969

To Dominic Olejniczak, President, and the
Board of Directors of the Green Bay Packers:

It is with sincere regret and after many hours of deliberation
that I am requesting a release from my contract with the Green
Bay Packers.

This was not only a difficult decision, but a highly emotional
one. I have made many close friends in Green Bay and in Wisconsin. Many of these are among the Board of Directors and the
Executive Committee. I sincerely hope we will continue in that
friendship.

My decision was based upon a number of factors. One was the
equity position with the Washington Redskins and I do not believe
I need go into the advantages of a capital gain position under
today's tax laws.

The other factor was really altruistic in that I need a challenge
and I have found the satisfaction of a challenge is not in main-
taining a position, but rather in attaining it. I can no more
walk away from this challenge than I could have walked away from
the one ten years ago. I am the same man today I was ten years
ago.

The future of the Packers is in good hands; the front office,
ticket office and the football field. The Packers have a good
football coach who will be a better one without the pressure
of having Vince Lombardi looking over his shoulder and without
the players wondering how the man upstairs might have done it.

MEMBER CLUB NATIONAL FOOTBALL LEAGUE • ELEVEN TIMES WORLD CHAMPIONS
WESTERN DIVISION CHAMPIONS 1938-1960 • SUPER BOWL CHAMPIONS 1966-1967

Each of us, if we would grow must be committed to excellence
and the victory, even though we know complete victory cannot be
attained, it must be pursued with all of ones might. The Championships, the money, the color; all of these things linger only
in the memory. It is the spirit, the will to excell, the will
to win; these are the things that endure. These are the important things and they will always remain in Green Bay.

There has never been a question of remuneration. After making
a decision a year ago not to coach, I think you all can well
understand the impossibility of my returning to the field in
Green Bay. It would be totally unfair to coaches and players
alike.

I have spent ten happy years in Green Bay. I know I will miss
the city, the team, but most of all, my friends.

                              Sincerely,

                              Vince Lombardi

VL:lsk

Lombardi's year in the Green Bay front office seems to have been a very unsettling time for all concerned. He turned over the team to Phil Bengtson, his long-time lieutenant and defensive coordinator, and took up office as an executive. But Lombardi didn't really know what to do with himself. He wanted to be on the field, but knew that being there could easily undermine the mild-mannered Bengtson. He became a spook, occasionally haunting practices from a discreet distance. "I didn't notice his presence much except game day," former guard Gale Gillingham says. "He talked to me before games quite a few times that year, but not in the same way as when he was coaching. He was very encouraging that year."

Not everyone appreciated the change. Defensive end Willie Davis, a long-time team captain and protégé of Lombardi's, just couldn't get used to the old man's new role. "It was totally strange, totally uncomfortable," Davis says. "I remember one day talking with him about it. He was stand-

ing out on the field, he was there a couple minutes, then went back upstairs to his office. He asked me to stop by. He said, 'Willie, one of the things that this year has taught me is that my real place in football is as a coach. Contracts and all that stuff, that's not me.' He said, 'I was born to coach.' "

If Lombardi was having a rough time of it, the Packers weren't doing much better. Bengtson was a brilliant defensive coach, but he didn't have Lombardi's forceful personality. Some players thought he was too soft on them, especially the graybeards who remembered Lombardi's kindhearted and ineffectual predecessor, Scooter McLean. Bengtson also happened to inherit an aging team, and it quickly went downhill. The '68 Packers had only one two-game winning streak, and they finished 6-7-1, their first losing record since Lombardi had arrived in 1959.

Davis remembers talking to his road roommate, Jerry Kramer, about the situation. Kramer said something had been missing all season—Lombardi's booming baritone

ABOVE Lombardi in 1968. He never got comfortable with his off-field role as general manager.

voice. It was a voice that could twist your insides in knots or immediately disarm you with a hoarse laugh. "I couldn't agree with him more," Davis says. "We kept waiting for that voice: 'C'MON, LET'S GO!!' Just the voice alone, the inflection and the tone of it. Phil was more laid back, maybe more cautious toward us. He was a great coach. I loved the man, and for ten years he made football very special to me at Green Bay on the defense. But I tell you, whether it was defense or offense, Lombardi was the man."

Packers fans probably saw what was coming. Even during the glory years they had lived with a vague fear that the native Easterner in their midst would return to his roots. Sure enough, Lombardi began to entertain the notion of moving on. "When I retired a year ago, I certainly had no intention of going back into coaching," he later explained to the Green Bay *Post-Crescent*. "It was a truthful retirement. It wasn't six months after I decided to retire that I realized I had made a bad decision. But as far as Green Bay is concerned, there was no way I could come back to coach here without hurting a lot of people."

Lombardi loved the strategies of coaching, the cat-and-mouse games of the chalkboard. He loved the excitement of Sundays in the NFL. And though he may not have admitted it, he soaked in the adulation he had received from the press and fans. But what eventually drove Lombardi back to the sidelines was what most football people miss when they leave the game—the bonds among men working for a common goal.

"There's a great closeness to a football team, you know—a rapport between the men and the coach that's like no other sport," he told *Sports Illustrated*. "It's a binding together, a knitting together. For me, it's like father and sons, and that's what I missed. I missed players coming up to me and saying, 'Coach, I need some help because my baby's sick,' or, 'Mr. Lombardi, I want to talk to you about trouble I'm having with my wife.' That's what I missed most. The closeness."

Still, Lombardi bided his time. The San Francisco 49ers had made a run at him after the 1967 season but were rebuffed.

He said no to the Boston Patriots, the Philadelphia Eagles, and the Pittsburgh Steelers, too. And then he said yes.

At the end of January, 1969, Lombardi addressed the Packers' directors at an Italian supper club called the Forum. In a private dining room the owners had named the Lombardi Room, the legendary coach informed his bosses that he was leaving for Washington, D.C. Vince Lombardi would be the head coach, executive vice president, and part owner of the Redskins. Lombardi had five years remaining on his contract, and the board of directors could have made it hard on him. They didn't. After a fierce internal debate among club leadership, he was released from his contract with no demands for compensation from the Redskins.

Lombardi got a sweetheart deal from his new team: $100,000 a year in salary and a five-percent share of the Redskins worth about $500,000—though his stock could be bought back at any given time. "I don't need the money," he insisted. "Money I've got. I need to coach!"

Lombardi had been a sporting-world footnote when he came to Green Bay in 1959, and his arrival was treated mainly as a curiosity. When the revered coach went to D.C. a decade

ABOVE The new coach of the Washington Redskins drills his players at Georgetown University in 1969.

149

ABOVE Long a national icon, Lombardi was hailed as a hero in Washington.

later, it was as if Charles Lindbergh had landed in Paris. In a city jaded by political power and headline makers, crowds turned to stare at the new coach when he walked down the street. When Redskins owner Edward Bennett Williams took Lombardi for a power lunch at Duke Zeibert's, the other patrons rose for a standing ovation. Then it was off to the Sheraton–Carlton Hotel, where more than 200 reporters and photographers had gathered in the Chandelier Room for Lombardi's first press conference. He strode to the podium and said, "Gentlemen, it is not true that I can walk across the Potomac River—not even when it is frozen."

Williams vacated his big office for Lombardi, and the new coach set about revamping the Redskins. Like the pre-Lombardi Packers, they were mired in a deep state of mediocrity. The Redskins hadn't had a winning season in fourteen years, hadn't tasted the playoffs in twenty-four. And they were without a first-round draft choice, having traded it to the Rams.

Lombardi was realistic about the challenges, and he fretted about his team's commitment. In notes he jotted down in July, he wrote, "Team not responding, offensively or defensively. Not reacting to pressure. My job to increase that pressure."

The Redskins thought their new coach was fiery enough, but those who knew him in Green Bay swore he had mellowed. One of them was Bob Long, a flanker whom Lombardi lured to Washington. "For example, we had a great tight end named Jerry Smith, a great pass catcher," Long told Gary D'Amato for the *Stadium Stories: Green Bay Packers*. "Well, he had long hair and Lombardi put up with it. In Green Bay you didn't have long hair. Lombardi was changing with the times a little bit."

The new boss did inherit some talent. In addition to Smith and Charley Taylor as pass catchers, he had the gifted if unbridled Sonny Jurgensen at quarterback, and he drafted a fine running back in Kansas State's Larry Brown, a steal in the eighth round. Lombardi also had a strong defensive

ABOVE D.C. mayor Walter Washington presents keys to the city to Lombardi and Senators baseball manager Ted Williams.

core in linebacker Chris Hanburger and defensive backs Pat Fischer and Brig Owens. Linebacker Sam Huff, an acquaintance from years ago in New York, came out of retirement to play for Lombardi. And like clockwork, Washington got better, finishing the season 7-5-2.

Still, Lombardi seemed unsure of his predicament. In his book *The Essential Vince Lombardi*, Vincent Jr. tells of riding in a car with his father when the older man turned to him and said, "You think I made a mistake taking this job, don't you?"

"To tell the truth, I hadn't thought about it one way or the other, but the question indicated to me that he had his own doubts," Lombardi Jr. writes.

In May of 1970, Coach Lombardi made what would turn out to be his final visit to Wisconsin. He returned to address state insurance underwriters in a Milwaukee hotel, and wound up chastising anti-war protestors for their lack of civility. The next day, he made a visit to Green Bay. According to the *Post-Crescent*, when someone asked him why he wouldn't come back to the city that still idolized him,

Lombardi replied, "I would like to, but . . . " And was too overcome with emotion to finish.

But Lombardi was in fine form when he played a round of golf. "I feel wonderful," he assured onlookers. It was a front. The coach was suffering from severe problems with his stomach, bowels, and kidneys, and they quickly grew worse. By June 24, 1970, Lombardi had checked into Georgetown University Hospital, where doctors would first find a lesion, then diagnose cancer in the rectal area of the colon.

It was a voracious carcinoma, and Lombardi steadily lost energy. Annoyed by a brewing NFL labor strike, he attended an owners' meeting in New York on July 21, but the trip took a lot out of him. He began radiation treatments on July 30, and passed away on September 3.

The phone calls and telegrams poured in both during Lombardi's illness and afterward, to his family. Even the NFL Players Association, an organization he had often sparred with, sent him a huge bouquet of flowers when he was in the hospital. The coach was buried at Mount Olivet cemetery in Middletown Township, New Jersey.

Lombardi's swift exit left the football world in shock. But his impact would be felt for years.

In a narrow sense, he lived on in NFL coaching circles. Several of Lombardi's former players became coaches. Bart Starr and Forrest Gregg both would coach the Packers (Gregg would lead the Cincinnati Bengals, too, and take them to Super Bowl XVI), and players such as Zeke Bratkowski and Boyd Dowler settled into long careers as assistants. "You can't clone a personality," Dowler says. "But his principles, his attention to detail—do things right all the time, develop day-to-day consistency."

"Discipline is the key word," Gregg says. "Without discipline, a team is not a team. As far as having the game change, it changed a great deal from the time I was playing to the time I was coaching the Bengals in the Super Bowl. But that part didn't change."

Less than a decade after Lombardi's death, the NFL instituted rules limiting a defensive back's contact on a

ABOVE Lombardi on the sidelines with quarterback Sonny Jurgensen in 1969. **OPPOSITE** Tributes to greatness, including the Vince Lombardi (Super Bowl) Trophy and the Lombardi Award, given annually to the top lineman in college football.

WORLD CHAMPS
1961
PACKERS 37 - GIANTS 0

LOMBARDI AWARD
OUTSTANDING
COLLEGE LINEMAN
ROTARY CLUB OF HOUSTON · AMERICAN CANCER SOCIETY

THE LOMBARDI CREDO

receiver, and allowing offensive linemen to extend their arms in pass blocking. It ushered in an era of passing and made Bill Walsh's West Coast offense possible—as well as the defensive reactions to it, primarily zone blitzes.

In effect, the current game looks quite a bit different than the brand they played in the 1960s, making film of Lombardi's offense look almost quaint. Bratkowski says that during his days as an assistant coach, few of his peers approached him to learn about the Lombardi system, treating the old man's disciples as "dinosaurs." He thinks they missed the point. "People always say, 'Well, the game may have passed him by,'" Bratkowski notes. "That's incorrect. He would have followed up with what's going on now and made adjustments."

Jerry Burns, Lombardi's defensive backs coach during his final two seasons in Green Bay, believes the weekly in-season schedule now common to NFL teams originated with the New York Giants of late 1950s, and was handed down by Lombardi and Tom Landry. "You could go from one team to another in the NFL right now, and the practice schedule would be almost exactly the same—Tuesday off, Friday is special teams, Saturday you have a walk-through and work on goal line," Burns says.

Anyway, Lombardi's legacy has a wider application. The coach was never simply an illustrator of Xs and Os. He had a genius for organization, for motivation, even philosophy. America recognized it, which is why Lombardi became so popular in circles that had nothing to do with football. Former tight end Ron Kramer can still dredge up many the coach's famed aphorisms. Among his favorites is, "Winning is not a sometime thing. It's an all the time thing."

"He used to say, 'You run a football team no differently than you run an army or a political party or a business,'" Kramer recalls. "The principle is the same. The objective is to win, to beat the other guy. It sounds cruel, but I don't think it is. And he worked as hard or harder than anybody."

Maybe that's one reason many of those old Packers did so well after football. Starr wound up as chairman of a

medical realty company. Willie Davis built a small empire of beverage distribution and radio stations. Carroll Dale is an assistant vice chancellor at the University of Virginia's College at Wise.

Davis recalls the chairman of a major corporation telling him of the indelible impression Lombardi's lessons had made on him—secondhand, via Davis. "I'll tell you right now, Lombardi was absolutely an unusual, exceptional, and unique guy," Davis says. "I played with Paul Brown for two years, I played for Eddie Robinson down at Grambling, and all these individuals had an impact on my life and I can remember and accord something to all of them. But no one—and I repeat, no one—was more of an impact on my life than Vince Lombardi."

And no one was more of an impact on the concepts of football, or the way coaches teach it to their players. Which is why, nearly forty years after his death, Lombardi remains synonymous with the game he loved.

OPPOSITE The man with the .750 overall winning percentage, the highest ever among NFL coaches. ABOVE Lombardi still presides over Lambeau Field, the stadium his Packers made iconic in the 1960s.

155

Bibliography

Carlson, Chuck. *Game of My Life*, Sports Publishing LLC, 2007.

Carroll, Bob et al. *Total Football II*, HarperCollins, 1999.

Current Biography, the H.W. Wilson Co., Vol. 24, No. 5, (May 1963).

Daley, Art. "Things Were Either 'Just Wonderful' or 'Just Terrible' for Emotional Vince," *Green Bay Post-Crescent*, Sept. 3, 1970.

D'Amato, Gary. *Stadium Stories: Green Bay Packers*. Globe Pequot Press, 2004.

Fimrite, Ron. "A Team for All Time," *Sports Illustrated*, Jan. 27, 1986.

Gifford, Frank. "A posthumous biography of Lombardi proves to be a moving, truthful statement," *Sports Illustrated*, Dec. 7, 1970.

Green Bay Packers Media Guide, 2007.

Hartnett, Ken. "Lombardi Preached on Life," *Green Bay Post-Crescent*, Sept. 3, 1970.

Johnson, William. "Arararararargh!" *Sports Illustrated*, Mar. 3, 1969.

"Lombardi," NFL Films, 1968.

Lombardi, Vince Jr. *The Essential Vince Lombardi*, McGraw-Hill, 2003.

Maraniss, David. *When Pride Still Mattered*, Simon & Schuster, 1999.

Maule, Tex. "The Day of Devastation," *Sports Illustrated*, Jan. 8, 1962.

———."Green Bay Packers," *Sports Illustrated*, Sept. 13, 1965.

———."The Green Crusher," *Sports Illustrated*, Sept. 19, 1966.

———."Bread-and-Butter Packers," *Sports Illustrated*, Jan. 23, 1967.

———."Green Bay, Handily," *Sports Illustrated*, Jan. 22, 1968.

Remmel, Lee. "Awesome Legend Unparalleled," *Green Bay Post-Crescent*, Sept. 3, 1970.

Riffenburgh, Beau. *The Official NFL Encyclopedia*, New American Library, 1986.

Rubin, Bob. *Green Bay Packers: Return to Glory*, Prentice-Hall, 1973.

Sharnik, Morton H. "Green Bay Blocks to Win," *Sports Illustrated*, Sept. 7, 1964.

Strother, Shelby. *NFL Top 40*, Viking, 1988.

Torinus, John B. *The Packer Legend*, Laranmark Press, 1982.

Wiebusch, John. *Lombardi*, Follett Publishing, 1971.

Wiebusch, John (ed). *The Super Bowl*, Simon & Schuster, 1990.

Vince Lombardi on Football, Vols. I and II, George Flynn (editor), New York Graphic Society and Wallynn Inc., 1973.

75 Seasons, Phil Barber (editor), Turner Publishing, 1994.

ABOVE The coach in a moment of repose on the sidelines, c. 1960.

Image Credits

Every effort has been made to trace copyright holders. If any unintended omissions have been made, becker&mayer! would be pleased to add appropriate acknowledgments in future editions.

Front cover: Vernon Biever/NFL

Page 2: Vernon Biever/NFL

Page 6: AP Photo/Martin Cohn

Page 8: Bettmann/CORBIS

Page 9: Courtesy of the Green Bay Packers Hall of Fame

Page 10: Courtesy of the Green Bay Packers Hall of Fame

Page 11: Courtesy of the Green Bay Packers Hall of Fame

Page 12: James Flores/NFL

Page 13: Courtesy of the Green Bay Packers Hall of Fame

Page 14: (top) Gerald R. Brimacombe/Time Life Pictures/ Getty Images (bottom)

Page 15: Courtesy of the Green Bay Packers Hall of Fame

Page 16: Courtesy of the Green Bay Packers Hall of Fame

Page 17: Courtesy of the Green Bay Packers Hall of Fame

Page 18: Bristol City Museum and Art Gallery, UK / The Bridgeman Art Library

Page 19: Courtesy of the Green Bay Packers Hall of Fame

Page 20: Courtesy of the Green Bay Packers Hall of Fame

Page 21: Courtesy of the Green Bay Packers Hall of Fame

Page 22: Courtesy of the Green Bay Packers Hall of Fame

Page 24: Courtesy of the Green Bay Packers Hall of Fame

Page 25: Courtesy of the Green Bay Packers Hall of Fame

Page 26: Kidwiler Collection/Diamond Images/ Getty Images

Page 27: Robert Riger/Getty Images

Page 28: Herbert Weitman/NFL

Page 29: Hy Peskin/Sports Illustrated/Getty Images (top); Herb Scharfman/Sports Imagery/Getty Images (bottom)

Page 30: Courtesy of the Green Bay Packers Hall of Fame

Page 32: Courtesy of the Green Bay Packers Hall of Fame

Page 33: Courtesy of the Green Bay Packers Hall of Fame

Page 35: Robert Riger/Getty Images

Page 36: Vernon Biever/NFL

Page 37: Robert Riger/Getty Images

Page 38: Robert Riger/Getty Images

Page 39: Courtesy of the Green Bay Packers Hall of Fame

Page 42: Courtesy of the Green Bay Packers Hall of Fame

Page 43: Courtesy of the Green Bay Packers Hall of Fame

Page 44: NFL Photos/Getty Images

Page 45: Robert Riger/Getty Images

Page 46: Courtesy of the Green Bay Packers Hall of Fame

Page 47: AP Photo

Page 48: Herbert Weitman/NFL

Page 49: Courtesy of the Green Bay Packers Hall of Fame

Page 50: Russ Russell/NFL (top) NFL/WireImage.com (bottom)

Page 53: Courtesy of the Green Bay Packers Hall of Fame

Page 54: Courtesy of the Green Bay Packers Hall of Fame

Page 55: Robert Riger/Getty Images

Page 56: Kidwiler Collection/Diamond Images/Getty Images

Page 57: Courtesy of the Green Bay Packers Hall of Fame

Page 58: Courtesy of the Green Bay Packers Hall of Fame

Page 59: Courtesy of the Green Bay Packers Hall of Fame

Page 60: Robert Riger/Getty Images

Page 63: Tony Tomsic/Getty Images

Page 64: Courtesy of the Green Bay Packers Hall of Fame

Page 65: Courtesy of the Green Bay Packers Hall of Fame

Page 66: Courtesy of the Green Bay Packers Hall of Fame

Page 67: Courtesy of the Green Bay Packers Hall of Fame

Page 68: Robert Riger/Getty Images

Page 69: Marvin E. Newman/Sports Illustrated/Getty Images

Page 70: Walter Iooss Jr./Sports Illustrated/Getty Images

Page 71: Vernon Biever/NFL

Page 72: Courtesy of the Green Bay Packers Hall of Fame

Page 73: Courtesy of the Green Bay Packers Hall of Fame

Page 74: Robert Riger/Getty Images

Page 75: Courtesy of the Green Bay Packers Hall of Fame

Page 76: Courtesy of the Green Bay Packers Hall of Fame

Page 77: Bettmann/CORBIS

About the Author

Phil Barber has covered sports, especially professional football, for twenty years. As a senior editor for NFL Publishing, a freelance writer, and, most recently, a reporter for California's *Santa Rosa Press Democrat*, he has approached the game from many angles. Barber spent seven years with the NFL, editing and writing for an array of projects, everything from coffee-table books to magazines to trading cards. He was the primary editor of *GameDay* magazine for three years and the annual Super Bowl program for two.

As a freelancer, Barber became a regular contributor to the *Sporting News*, where he consulted with coaches and scouts to expose the chalkboard strategy underlying the sport of football. He continued to write for NFL publications, as well as *Sports Illustrated* and the *San Francisco Chronicle*. He also contributed non-sports stories to magazines including *Bon Appetit*, the *Los Angeles Times Magazine*, *Air & Space*, and *NurseWeek*. Barber has covered the Oakland Raiders beat for the *Press Democrat* since 2003, writing for both the print and online editions of the paper while continuing his freelance work for the *Sporting News*. He has authored or co-authored twelve books, including *We Were Champions: The 49ers' Dynasty in Their Own Words*.

Acknowledgments

The author would like to acknowledge the assistance and guidance of Tom Murphy of the Green Bay Packers Hall of Fame, and Aaron Popkey of the Packers' public relations department. Also, much thanks to Jim Buckley of Shoreline Publishing, who helped connect me to this project, and to editor Amy Wideman and photo researcher Chris Campbell at becker&mayer!. Mostly, thanks to my wife, Kara Brunzell, and my daughters Ynez, Alice, Simone, and Nora, for understanding why I spent the better part of four months in my "office." As a quintet, they aren't as stout as Skoronski, Fuzzy, Ringo, Kramer, and Gregg, but they're a lot better looking.